Talking Memories

LIFE IN A SMALL VILLAGE

With best wishes
Tommy O'Reilly

- Thomas O'Reilly -

First Edition: October 2013

Copyright: Thomas O'Reilly©
2013

All Rights Reserved.
No part of this publication may be reproduced or transmitted in any form or
by any means, whether mechanical, recording or any information storage or
retrieval system, without the prior written consent of the publisher.

ISBN 978-0-9927033-0-1

9 780992 703301 >

PUBLISHED BY: THOMAS O'REILLY

PRINTED BY JETPRINT, TULLAMORE, CO. OFFALY.
TEL: 057 9341373

ACKNOWLEDGEMENTS

This work required the help of many individuals.
A special note of gratitude to Annette Doolan who faithfully
typed out and corrected a major part of the work.

Thanks to the following people:-

Bridie Flynn who read the first draft;
Ralph Loomis and Breda Campion for subsequent
readings and suggestions made;
Noel Foynes who offered valuable suggestions;
The people interviewed - for their great memories;
Jackie O'Connell, Joe O'Sullivan and the people who kindly
loaned photographs;
Laois Partnership Company for their support.

Other books by Thomas O'Reilly

Severino -
a play translated and adapted from the poem
Morte e Vida Severina by Joao Cabral de Melo Neto

An Acre Sown

Cover is a painting of Clonaslee by Noel McMahon which was
kindly loaned by John Flanagan. Noel McMahon never signed
his own name to his paintings but always signed with the
presence of a little dog.

FOREWORD

"The bicycles go by in twos and threes -
There's a dance in Billy Brennan's barn tonight"
                                                    Inniskeen Road: July Evening
                                                    Patrick Kavanagh

Patrick Kavanagh in his celebrated poem *Inniskeen Road: July Evening* captures more than most a very down-to-earth description of Irish country life in mid-twentieth century Ireland. This small snapshot of dance goers could have taken place in any part of rural Ireland. Very similarly, this excellently written book *Talking Memories* is also a portrayal of life in a rural setting from the mid-twentieth century to the present. It is based around locality or as in the words of American novelist Gertrude Stein: *"this is the place of places, and it is here."*

Local history has been defined as the study of history in a geographically local context as it concentrates on the local community. It incorporates the cultural and social aspects of history. Local histories are more often than not recorded as oral tales or stories. Local histories have been less documented than national or continental histories with fewer books available thus making this publication all the more significant for its recording of memories that over time have become woven into the fabric of a local identity.

In the pages of *Talking Memories - Life in a Small Village*, Father O'Reilly has managed to meticulously capture the essence of this identity. As a local history it involves the two essential elements of people and place, it addresses the nuts and bolts of how this community got to this point and, to a greater or lesser extent, how we might get to the next. The central themes in his work are the stories of a people in this unique place and of their personal links to the larger community of county and nation. As one reads on it becomes apparent as in the words of historian Thomas Carlyle that you are reading: *"the biography of the everyday people."* It constantly reminds us that history (and the responsibility for it) begins in our own surroundings.

As you explore further into this book you also gain a new insight and perspective into the issues that mattered to each of the people interviewed.

Scottish author and dramatist J.M. Barrie held that: *"God gave us memory so that we might have roses in December."* These individual recollections celebrate not only the memories of family and friends but also of so many momentous local events such as Rural Electrification, Group Water Schemes, the building of the Vocational School, the setting up of Clonaslee Co-operative Society and to the ever increasing love affair with the motor car. Socially and educationally not forgotten were the roles played by the ICA and the Macra na Feirme night classes which taught the importance of leadership in a rural setting from another era.

To Father O'Reilly, we extend a very deep sense of thanks and gratitude from the entire community for your painstaking work so honestly and patiently undertaken over a long period and appropriately published to coincide with the bi-centenary celebrations of St. Manman's Church. It has resulted in a vibrant work that has dealt with the surroundings, the environment, and the people of this place and how they felt. It has recorded its findings and conclusions in a meaningful narrative.

It has successfully linked the past to the present always mindful that: *"if you want to understand today, you have to search yesterday."*

The readers of this book now and in time to come both at home and abroad will appreciate forever its significance for this community.

> *"History cannot give us a programme for the future,*
> *but it can give us a fuller understanding of ourselves,*
> *and of our common humanity,*
> *so that we can better face the future."*
>
> Robert Penn Warren

Noel Foynes
September 2013

PREFACE

Each morning Tom Higgins drove into Clonaslee where he discussed the village and nations events in Moran's Shop on Main Street. On our first meeting he brought me on a tour of the village, pointing out who lived on Main Street, going up the left hand side to the Heritage Centre, which was formerly the Church of Ireland. We then came down the other side stopping at the bridge over the Clodiagh River. The following evening we continued the journey as he pointed out the Parochial Hall, the Court House, now a dwelling house, around the Green, back down Chapel Street and the Tullamore Road. As we ended our journey for the evening, he remarked how there were nine in the parish over the age of ninety and *"I'm glad to be one of them"*.

Over the past six years Tom and twenty five others have allowed me to interview them and tell me their stories. Some of them have since passed away. The outreach and influence of their lives was to go beyond the boundaries of Clonaslee and its surrounding areas.

This book is a look back at the history of Clonaslee over those years. Their memories, the ventures they undertook and the life they lived. Each contributed to a way of life that appears now to be a thing of the past, but not such a distant past.

It has been a worthwhile and rewarding time. I hope their contributions will give some insight into life in Clonaslee over the years.

Thomas O'Reilly, January 2013

DEDICATION

Talking Memories

LIFE IN A SMALL VILLAGE

Dedicated to the people of Clonaslee, Co. Laois

CONTENTS

Tom Higgins

Ninety Years

TOM HIGGINS, BROCCA

Where I am living now I was born. I am here all my life since 1917. I had no brother and four sisters. The oldest of the girls, Sarah is a nun in New York. She left here about 1936. She was younger than me. She was born in 1919. She went to the ordinary school here in Clonaslee and then she went to school in Portarlington staying with an aunt. One day a nun came to the Convent and got a couple of girls to join the nuns. The first place she went to was a convent this side of Mullingar. It is now a hotel, Bloomfield. She was there in the convent until about 1938 and then she was sent to Italy. She remained in Italy until the war started and then she was sent to New York. She has remained there all this time. She was last home six years ago, in 2001. A girl who went to school with her in Clonaslee is now in New York, one of the Blake's up on the mountain. She is alive still and is also a nun.

I walked in to school every day from Brocca. A crowd of us went together and came home together. My mother brought me the first day in the pony and trap. There were two teachers in the school. A lady teacher from Tullow in Carlow, Miss Foley, who later married Frank Dunne who lived by the side of the Priest's field, now the GAA Park. The priest had a horse and used to graze him there. The priest's name was Father Murray. For three years I went to Miss Foley's room in the school and then I went into Mr Hennessy's room. He was the Principal and was from Erril in County Laois. He lived just outside the village at Gorrough Bridge. The house is still there. It was nice when we had that old man teaching us until he retired. The man that came after him was John Bates, father of Paddy and Fran Bates. He was a Laois man. He was a single man and hurled on the Clonaslee team. I got on well with him. He used to put up a prize for the lessons before the summer holidays. The prizes were for reading, writing, and everything in the school. The number of pupils going to school then was about ninety. When we went into Third Class, in the other room, half were sitting in desks writing and the other half were standing up reading. The school was cold in the winter but each pupil brought a load of turf. There was one pupil who never had to bring a load of turf. His house was beside the school. His name was Paddy Morris. He always brought the "live" sod of turf to light the fire. That house in Chapel Street is gone now, not even ruins. Kathleen Murphy lives where the school was.

Tom Higgin's aunts and sisters.
Back L-R: Aunt Rose, Aunt Tilly, Aunt Bridie, Aunt Margaret.
Front L-R: Julia Higgins, Sister Patricia, Cis Dunne.

Nearly all of my classmates are now dead. The school inspector nearly always came once a year along with the Religious Inspector who was Father Carey. There was always great preparation for the visit of the Inspectors. Everybody had to be in school those days.

One of my classmates, Sean Conroy of Tinnahinch was a Christian Brother for years. Later on he became a priest and is now in America.

Several times I rode my bike to matches in Croke Park. The first time I went on my own and I stopped on the Quays in a Bed and Breakfast. I got up the next morning went to Mass in a big church on the Quays, came to the house and got my breakfast. Laois were playing Kildare in football. I rode my bike down to Croke Park, parked under the Hogan Stand, and went into the match. Laois won by two points. A few minutes before the match was over I got my bike, rode down to Naas where I got something to eat. I got home about 10 o'clock Sunday night. There was no 'Match of the Day' then.

I brought my lunch in my school bag along with my books. At the beginning I was in the Infants Class. At that time there were more people living in the country places than in the village. So a crowd of us went to school every day. In the summertime a lot of them went to school in their bare feet. The Caseys and the Flynns went to school with me. They lived a mile down below me in Cush. They would pass by my house and they would shout if I wasn't out. When I was going to school there were thirteen Church of Ireland people on the road. Now there are none. There were seven of a family in Lees and one man in Coltons, one in Killart House called Willie Vough. There were two in Fawcetts, husband and wife. There were two Jessops, husband and wife.

The Caseys were big strong fellas. There were three boys and three girls. They are all dead. Living next to them were the Flynns, four boys and three girls, all now dead. The Flynns are all gone as well as their house while in the Caseys there is Mary Bridget Dunne from Ballymacrory who married the youngest boy Tom. Their son lives there now with Mrs Casey.

My lunch at school each day was two cuts of cake bread, homemade bread with butter and sometimes jam. This was our own butter, which my mother made at home. I can remember churning the milk until it turned into butter. The butter was made every Monday as I said, I helped with the churning and the butter which was leftover was put into pound rolls and brought into Tullamore. It was sold in the market every Tuesday along with the eggs. I drove the pony and trap with my mother and the money from the eggs and butter brought home the groceries for the week. There were a lot of small shops in Tullamore all gone now. My parents would not recognise Tullamore now. If we were short anything we went to Clonaslee but there was also bread vans going by and we stopped them and bought bread if we were short.

- *Talking Memories* -

In school we got out at half twelve, we ate our lunch and we hurled either on the road or on the green. We usually cut an ash tree with a nice turn on it and made the hurley ourselves. We played with a rubber ball if we hadn't a hurling ball. We collected a penny each and that bought a leather hurling ball.

I had an Uncle Tom Higgins who played for Clonaslee and Laois. He played in the All-Ireland Final against Clare in 1914, before I was born. He got a puck on the back of the head and so missed playing for Laois in 1915 against Cork in the Final.

The school started at half past nine. We left my house at half past eight to get in to school by half nine. On a wet day we were often wringing wet when we got in.

We learned the Catechism first, then history. We had a schoolbook with stories in it. When the Inspector came he questioned us on this book. We also studied Geography, Irish and Sums. I liked Geography and History best of all.

I was ten years of age when my father died. He died in 1927. My mother died in 1972. My mother's maiden name was Holton. She was up from Gorrough - it means 'rough land'. All the houses up there, approximately twelve, are all unoccupied. The farthest person that lived up there was Jane Dunne - she was Jane Westman then. The majority of them are all dead.

My father was ailing for a year before he died. He was on the Tug-O-War team. A lot of them died early. It must have been all the pulling they did. I think they must have overdone it and this affected their hearts. I can remember my father's funeral even though I was only ten years old.

It was all horses and ponies at the funeral. The hearse was drawn by two horses. The undertaker was Joe Conroy of Clonaslee. He lived where McDermott's Public house is now. Joe Conroy and his brother-in-law sat up on the front of the hearse driving the two black horses. They were in long black coats and hard black hats. They had whips in their hands. This made a big impression on me. I was only ten, the oldest of five children. Sheila, my sister, the youngest was only three. The undertaker had a black mourning coach pulled by two horses; it could take five or six mourners. My mother and all of us came behind the hearse on the way to the Church.

The old Parish Priest, Father Fanning, loved to go the whole way to the graveyard in Kilmanman with somebody who had a good big trap. He was very fond of walking, but he liked a good trap to go to the funeral. He always went into the graveyard and said the De Profundis. Funerals took place at 2:30 pm at which there were offerings. These offerings were to help poor people to bury the dead and when they did not need them the offerings were given to the priest.

It was hard for my mother then as the price of cattle was very cheap and my mother had to pay someone to do the work. At

Photo taken five days after their father's death by Mai McGilton in August 1927. L-R: Maura, Tom and Sheila Higgins.

that time there were two masses on a Sunday, 8 am and 11 am. Weekday masses were usually at 8 am.

My mother reared pigs, cattle and all sorts of fowl. The food at the time was what we grew on the farm, potatoes, cabbage, turnips and bacon. We usually killed a pig. My mother made the bread and we had the milk from the cows. The only thing we had to buy was tea, sugar and flour. There was no chocolate and very little sweets. We always had porridge at night for our supper.

There was a big wake for everyone when they died. The rosary would be said about 11 pm. Nearly all the neighbours stopped all night at the wake. They got bread and tea, there were a couple of meals during the night. Every man got a clay pipe full of tobacco and he was to smoke that during the night. Refreshments were always served as well.

I can remember the 1930's when everything we had to sell was very cheap. We got hardly any money for anything. I remember going in to Tullamore, O'Connor Square to see De Valera. He gave a speech. I was able to hear him as I went in early to be up near the platform as there were no microphones in those days. At that time a ploughman earned ten shillings a week. The economic war was on and England would buy nothing from Ireland.

At the Fianna Fail Rally in Tullamore some of the big names of the day, Eamon Boland, Lar Brady, Paddy Gorry, from Kilcavan, Eamon Donnelly, from Banagher were all present. The square was full. De Valera promised that there would be better pay, more work and better prices which didn't always work out. After that the politician that made a great impression on me was Oliver J Flanagan. He came from Mountmellick. One day in the fair in Tullamore an old women came selling verses. One was about Oliver J.

Hurrah me boys for Oliver J
For Oliver J hurrah
He fears no foes
Where'er he goes
A first class lad is he
And a terror to Dail Eireann boys
Since 1943.

His party was Monetary Reform, his own party, and then he joined Fine Gael. He had a good gift of the gab - nowadays he would be termed a good communicator. He was a good man on the platform - which was important in those days. He travelled all over Laois and Offaly by bicycle. He was at all the funerals and was a local man from Mountmellick.

Nowaday all the streets and lanes are tarred. But I can remember when they were all rough and mostly stone.

I can remember everybody walking. I used to walk three miles across the fields to hurl on a Sunday down to Annaghmore. It means 'the big swamp'. There was a lake there. Most of our journey was through a wood until we came to Russells. That house is now down and nobody lives there. They got a divide of land from the Land Commission and built a new house on good land. The whole family are now dead five boys and one girl. Ger Russell, the sports commentator is a nephew of theirs. We hurled on Russell's field. We made a match between ourselves. There were about ten on each side.

The Russels always came to Mass in Clonaslee even though they were in Mount Bolus Parish. They had to come through a wood and in the wintertime it could be very wet. I often think of the hardship people had to go through to get to Mass and yet they never missed it. In the wintertime they had to wear big old boots, there was no rubber Wellingtons at the time. On their way, at a turf stack, they changed to shoes or fine boots. They hid the old boots in the turf stack. We used to hear them talking going by our house. My mother would shout *"There's the Russells gone to Mass, get up"*. We'd get a cup of tea. I would yoke up the pony and trap and when we got to the Church the Russells would be at the Church Gate. Where the Credit Union is now there was a little house and we used to put the pony and trap in there. Where the wall is now along by the River Clodiagh people tied their horses.

I got my first bicycle around 1930. It was bought in Tullamore. It was a Raleigh. I rode to Dublin a few times. Gradually more people got bikes. Sometime after that my sisters got bikes and rode to school in Tullamore. This was Secondary school as they already had been to the Girls' School in Clonaslee. We all learned how to mend a puncture, fixing it at home with a patch and solution.

The first car that came to the village belonged to Doctor Twomey and this was around 1924. It was a little two seater car and I'm not sure what make. An old man, he looked old to me, had a hackney car. This was for bringing people to Mass, shopping in Tullamore and any place they wanted to go. The petrol pumps were beside Egan's shop and the owners' name was Bryant. A family called Bourkes came from Dublin to live in Clonaslee in 1934. They lived in the Main Street and they had a Hackney car as well. Pat Bourke, the present undertaker is a descendant of theirs. Father Doyle came to Clonaslee about 1933 on a pushbike. Shortly after that he got a motor bike, the first in the village. He graduated to the motor bike as he found it easier going up the mountain to celebrate the Station Mass. Father Murray came here from Killeigh in 1914. He walked everyplace and usually got a lift in a pony and trap if he was going to a funeral.

In 1947 Father Murray fell asleep while reading the paper. He was reading the paper by candlelight and it caught fire. His clothes were burned and he was badly burned himself. He died shortly afterwards and is buried in the Chapel yard.

I got my first car in 1948. I bought it from Walshe's in Tullamore. It was an Anglia and cost £330 - an awful lot of money. Before I got my car I sat into Bourke's hackney car and drove it a few times. There were only three or four cars in the village. I got my first tractor in 1950. I went to Dublin and drove it home. It took me over six hours. I got the garage plates from Roberts in Tullamore, went to Dublin and brought it home. It was a Ferguson. It was around the same price as the car. It was hard on the tyres as the roads around my house were not tarred.

Tom Higgins at the gate to his house.

There are big changes in the village since my time going to school. There were about twenty five shops in it at that time and they were all doing business. Where Morans is now there were two men who used to make boots and shoes. Their names were Willie Gorman and his brother and they had a sister, a dressmaker. They all lived there together. After Morans was Dan McRedmond, he was a caretaker in the Water Works. He was the father of Donal, Jim and Blaise, who died recently. Bourkes had a draper shop close by. Then there was a Public House owned by Callaghans. Further on Joe Conroy had a Public House. He was the undertaker and he also sawed timber. Beside them was an old couple, Frank Kelly and his sister. Then there was Dunne's Public House. It is now Pooles. Next to that was the Church of Ireland School. The teacher was Mr Pattison followed by Mrs Webster, a daughter of his. She was before her time as she had a type of playschool for all denominations on Sunday mornings. It is now Blooms Restaurant. Next was William Bryant, he had a hackney car. He was a native of Killoughey. Egan's fine big shop was next.

The manager of the shop was Sean Mooney who came from Killeigh. He ended up his days on The Green. There were about three shop boys. One of them was Gus Ennis. I think he got a shop of his own down in Ballycumber after spending a good few years in Egans. Jim Sweeney was there for a good few years before he became Manager. He left here to relieve managers of other Egan branches at various times. It was a big shop selling groceries and hardware. Farther up the street there were three or four small houses and I forget the names of the people who lived in them.

Opposite Egans, on the other side of the main street, was Morrisseys. Billy Morrissey had one daughter Maureen. She married a schoolteacher by the name of Desmond Dillon. He was a woodwork teacher in the Technical School known as the Vocational School. Desmond Dillon came from Portlaoise. Morriseys sold drapery for everybody, men, women and children. He did a great business. Both he and Bourkes did great business on a Saturday night. I bought clothes in both shops as well as shopping in Tullamore. I bought many suits in Morrisseys. They took your measurements and made up the suit. Every suit then had a waistcoat. I don't know why it was called a waistcoat. The suit cost about five Irish pounds in the early 1940's. I bought boots and shoes in both drapery shops. I can't ever remember buying a tie but I must have bought one somewhere because I always wore one on a Sunday going to Mass. The suit and tie were taken off, hung up and not to be used again until the following Sunday. Next door to Morriseys was John Ewell, an elderly man living on his own. Mrs Eilish Maher, I think lives there now. A butcher's shop was next door belonging to Luke McRedmond. I think he died in Clonaslee and the next butcher I can remember was Dan Hickey in the Square and then Cyril Morris opened up beside Egans. Coming back down the street was Boland's Pub. When they died it was sold to Martin Fallon who came from Roscommon. They are still there. Next door was a family of

Hylands who have died out. I think they were from Rosenallis. Next to that is the Post Office. I remember four or five different families there. Miss Guinan was there when I was a young fellow. She came from Mountmellick. Next came Mrs Lawlor, Eilish Lawlor ran the post office. They also had groceries and hardware.

After the Post Office there was a tailor, Owen Dunne, he used to make suits. This is now part of the Post office. Beside the tailors was Callaghan's Draper Shop. Patsy Kelly opened a Fish and Chip shop and it is now known as Antonio's, who came to Clonaslee from Italy. There was a small shop located next door, which sold religious objects, belonging to Foynes, grandparents of the present family. There were several incumbents where Brickleys are now. I can remember soldiers there when I was going to school. There were sandbags around the doors as they were being attacked by the Black and Tans. It was a Guards' barracks at one stage. Peavoy's shop was next. I can remember three generations of the family living there - over a hundred years. Beside them were Troys who were stonecutters.

Guard Barry and his family lived where Edmund Dunne is living now in the Lodge. Guard Barry was transferred from Clonaslee to Portarlington and died there. Next house now is the Barracks. I remember it was burnt twice during my lifetime. The first time was in 1921. When I was going to school it was a ruin. The Black and Tans were blamed for it. It was re-built by Sweeneys of Portarlington in 1933. It was burnt again in 1975. This time the I.R.A. was blamed for it. It was again re-built to stand as it is today. Where Bourkes have the machinery shed now there was once a Public House. It was known as 'The Fox and Goose'. Daly's house was joining the old hall before they built the new house. The old hall still stands. At the back of the old hall was the Billiard Room, which is still there. Joining that was a grocery shop belonging to a man called William Moran. When he died it was left to his niece Josie Tynan. And when she died Selma

Sherlock bought it.

The house next door belonged to a Guard Lyons. Guard Lyons died and an only daughter married the Forestry ganger O'Mahoney. Next to that were four houses. Martin and Mary Anne Delaney lived there. They were grandparents of Eugene Doolan, who lives in Castlecuffe now but who originally came from Killoughey. Beside them was their son Morgan. He worked in the Forestry and died of a heart attack up on the Cut Road. Three of those houses were left to Cullitons of Brittas. They sold them at an auction to PJ Fitzpatrick, who knocked them down as they were about to crumble. They were all pulled down and so far no building has taken place on that site. The next building was The Courthouse. A family called Colgan lived in the courthouse. Three of them were unable to speak. When they died Sean Mooney bought the Courthouse. There were court sessions one day every month. One case I remember was the Kirwan Case - Bernie Kirwan from Rahan. It made 'National' headlines. Bernie Kirwan was accused of killing his brother. It was a gruesome case because of the manner in which he killed his brother and disposed of the body. He was found guilty in Tullamore Court after being referred there from Clonaslee.

The only house out the Birr Road was where the Catholic Curate lived. It is now occupied by Fergal and Fiona Conroy. Next came Edward Troy of Brittas.

Father Murray was Parish Priest when I was young. The Curate was Father Doyle. Father Murray lived where Hylands now

Tom Higgins at the Steam Rally.

live. They bought the Parochial House when Father Ryan was transferred as Parish Priest to Abbeyleix. Tom Higgins, my first cousin, lived where John and Nora Flynn live now. Our local dispensary was next door to Tom Horans. Nurse Curtis, who was also the maternity nurse, lived there. D.E. Williams of Tullamore had a bar and grocery in the Square. This changed hands a few times. Paul Brophy ran the business, replaced by Flynns and now Selma Sherlock. Where Tom Horan now lives belonged to Williams and the shop boys lived there.

Two sisters, Ellen and Mary Anne Dolan ran a Public House where Hickeys is now. Connells bought it from Dolans. They were from Offaly down near Geashill and Mary Connell who married Dan Hickey took over. Their daughter Mary now runs it with her brother Joe.

Michael Dolan, a brother of the two girls lived next door. Joe and Mary Quinn now live there. John Cusack was next door which is now occupied by Joe and Babs Young. Charlie Doolan and his sister Margaret lived where Eugene Conroy is. Two brothers and two sisters lived where Dinny and Betty Finnerty now live.

Passing the church entrance Michael McCabe, a carpenter, and his sister lived. They lived to be over a hundred. Paddy Farrell now lives there. Next to him was Matt Dunne, his wife and family. It is now vacant. Next to that was Morris. Tom Morris used to look after the Chapel. This brings me down to my old university, my old school, built in 1832. Before that school education was in the hedge school. Both boys and girls went there until the Girls School was built in 1909. The Boys school was built out the Mountmellick Road in 1951. Now they are both back together again.

A man from Killeigh lived next to the lane going up to the new school. Myra Sherlock, the hairdresser lives on that street. Before her there was a family call Mahons. Next is Ned Smith. He is there a long time. Frank Dunne married my first teacher Miss Foley from Carlow and they lived alongside Tom Smith. Then came the Credit Union, Padriag Byrne lives there now. His mother was a teacher in Tinnahinch.

During all my years farming at home where I still live I grew corn, sowed potatoes, vegetables and beet. I reared cattle, kept pigs and fowl. I kept six cows and sold the milk to the local creamery. I brought it myself for awhile every morning except Sundays, Jim Dunne of Ballymacrory had a lorry and he began bringing milk to the creamery and brought mine as well. My mother, my sisters and I did the milking each morning at 7:30 am. When my mother died we gave it up. After keeping cattle for about two years I brought them to the fair in Tullamore. Sometimes I sold some to the Murrays of Coolaboughlan. Times have changed as regards beet, as now the sugar factories are all closed. During the Second World War, I began sowing beet and delivered it to the Railway Station in Tullamore where it was brought down to Tuam in Co Galway.

During the economic war in the 1930's we got very little for the cattle. A calf was only worth five shillings and it hardly paid you to keep it but we had nothing else and tried to manage as best we could. We reared about four pigs at a time. Usually one was kept which we killed ourselves and the rest were brought up to the weighbridge in Clonaslee. Luke McRedmond, the butcher used to buy the pigs on a Monday. He stored the pigs, which were brought away that evening to the factory. The pig brought in about £5. Farming was a hard life. You were out in all weathers and it's the only work I ever knew. I started when my father died. As I said, I was only ten so I got an early apprenticeship. When times got better I bought a tractor. This enabled me to do some hire work as well as my own work on the farm.

There are about nine in the parish now who are over ninety and I'm glad to be one of them.

Jim Sweeney

Coupon 'G' and a Half Ounce of Tea

JIM SWEENEY, MAIN STREET

I was born in Tullamore Hospital in March 1919, so I am an Offaly man living in Laois. My parish was Kilcormac though at that time it was known as Frankford. I think it changed its name around 1919, the year I was born. Father O'Reilly was the Parish Priest and he may have changed it. The Parish Priests had a lot of power then.

- Talking Memories -

One of my earliest memories was the first day I went to the Convent School. A boy called Frankie Slevin brought me to school. He was in First Class, and used to pass my door everyday so my mother asked him to bring me along with him. A nun met us outside in the schoolyard, her name was Sister Magdalene. My memory is dim of my early years but I do remember playing with plasticine. I stayed with the nuns until First Communion and then I went to the Boys School, which was then outside the town. I stayed there until I was fourteen.

It was a two-teacher school. Edward Ryan was the Master and Miss Buckley was the Assistant. Looking back I have to say that it was a good period in my life and I enjoyed hurling on the school team. I can remember playing in goals against Ballyboy. Father Jennings, the Curate, put up a set of jerseys for the winning team. Kilcormac won the match. Father Jennings, after the match, felt it would not be fair if only one team got jerseys so he decided to give everyone a jersey. He gave a blue and white jersey to the Kilcormac boys and green and white jersey to the Ballyboy team. Looking back I think it was very generous of him. He was a very good singer, sang in concerts and later on went as Curate to Castlejordan.

When I got to Sixth Class I left school and began looking for a job. I applied to several places including P & H Egan and D.E. Williams of Tullamore. I had to go for an interview and an aunt of the Egans, Miss Bel Brown from Kilcormac recommended me. I got the job at the grocery counter measuring out stones of sugar, half pounds of tea, pounds of bread soda, pounds of rice, washing soda and sago.

So I began my working life at P & H Egan shop in my own town. At that time P & H Egan had seventeen shops in Laois, Offaly, Westmeath and Longford. They were a strong going concern and they had a branch here in Clonaslee. At the beginning I had the title of Relief Assistant. This meant working in different branches of the company, relieving people who were out sick or on holidays. The first branch I was sent to after Kilcormac was Castletown-Geoghegan in Co Westmeath. It's a village and would be smaller than Clonaslee. I was a short time there when I was transferred to Ferbane. I was transferred all over the place in a short space of time helping out here and there. From Ballycumber, I went to Tubber and I was there when the Second World War commenced. I can remember it well as I was doing Manager Relief at the time. The papers were delivered in bundles and I can remember reading on the heading of the *'Irish Press'*, *'Britain Declares War on Germany'*. As far as I remember, Mr Chamberlain was Prime Minister of England at the time. There was a great rumour about scarcities and people were coming into the shop and stocking up. All of us working there stayed with Mrs. Stones. We got all our meals there. We were paid £1, seven shillings and six pence a month indoors, Egans paying Mrs Stones for our food and accommodation. One day a man on a bicycle was going around selling clothes and I bought a pullover from him. It cost three shillings and sixpence.

I came to Clonaslee in late 1939. I stayed where I am living now with the manager of the Clonaslee branch, Sean Mooney and his wife. There was plenty of activity for a young fellow in Clonaslee. One could play billiards at night time in the Parochial Hall at The Green or I could go down to the GAA field to puck a ball around with other fellows. Travelling shows often came to the village so I was never bored and I had plenty to do each day in my job. The 'rationing' started when I was here. Sean Lemass, who was Minister for Supplies in the Fianna Fail De Valera led government, announced that due to the war there would be two ounces of tea per person per week. That particular week he later announced it would be reduced to half an ounce per week. Sugar was rationed, each person getting a half pound per week. Eventually everything was rationed. Every household was supplied with ration books for each person in the house. It is hard for people nowadays to understand this, as now there is no shortage of food or clothes.

In each ration book there were pages of coupons. For instance, the coupon "G" would entitle you to half an ounce of tea. We kept a register of all our customers and marked them off each month when they came in for their 'rations' of tea, sugar, butter, flour, soap and paraffin oil. Even to buy clothes one needed coupons. Today's teenagers would be forgiven in not understanding how difficult it was to buy a garment. I bought a sports coat one time and there was no lining in it. The shop assistant told me he would get it later on but I don't remember ever getting it.

Life was difficult in the shop as people came in and claimed that they hadn't got their rations. Bread was a big problem at that time. Some weeks families got six loaves, the following week three, depending on how supplies came in. So we had to ration them out to our customers. No such thing as going in to a shop and selecting whatever brand of bread you liked. The bread was mostly black made up of the whole wheat and consequently less flour. I never saw bananas or oranges during the war. There was hardly any chocolate or sweets. Christmas was a terrible time as each shop got a quota of raisins and sultanas. Customers were very upset, as they never got enough to make Christmas cakes and Christmas puddings. It is hard to believe now that bacon, rashers, and black puddings were so scarce. Takeaways and Deli counters along with fast food outlets were not even dreamt of. Each loaf of bread that you sold represented coupons. They had to be handed into the Bakery to get more.

There was no electricity then and no sewerage. There was no running water. Water had to be drawn from pumps and wells and we also had the river. There was a well and pump in Egan's yard. The public could come and take water home in buckets. We used oil and tilley lamps in the shop. The first job in the morning was to clean the lamps and trim the wicks. Then we had to sweep the floor. It was a cement floor with a patch of wood behind the counter. It was warmer to stand there. And of course, it was a wooden counter. The doors opened at 8.30 am. I got a break from 1-2 pm during which I had dinner. The shop closed at 10 pm so the second part of the day was the longest. The Government made a compulsory order that there should be a half day every week. Most shops closed on a Wednesday afternoon. One facility that the village lacked was a Chemist Shop and it is still the same today. Part of my work was doing deliveries. People ordered commodities in the shop and I delivered them on a carrier bike. I also used a hand truck around the town.

Half-days I usually cycled home to Kilcormac. It took about an hour, hail, rain or snow as the saying goes. Usually I had a bicycle lamp. You could be stopped by the Guards if you had no light on your bike. After a year in Clonaslee, I went as Manager to Foighla in Co Longford. I was the youngest Manager ever appointed in the firm. Foighla was only a crossroads. Ballymahon was three miles away. Keenagh was a village close by. The man that I replaced was Pat Dunne, a Cavan man, who went to work in the Ardagh branch. Aaron Egan came in every day and used to get our meals. There were two Bourke brothers who worked in the shop as well. I spent 4 years there in charge. It wasn't as busy as Clonaslee but there was a bar attached to the Grocery. This meant that we stayed open until about 11.30 pm. Of course people who lived further than three miles had a right to be served under the Bona Fide law. So it could be the next morning before one got to bed. The Guards now and again came by but we were always able to get the locals out the back door if required.

I remember Eskrine Childers, who was one of the local T.D.s, later he became President of Ireland. I met him outside

Clough Church, a few miles away. The Parish Priest, Father Maguire, asked me to introduce him to the people at an election rally after Mass. He was looking for votes as an election was coming up. I wasn't attached to any particular party but I was involved with them all through the shop and business. As I was introducing him to the crowd, some people heckled him. This was par for the course as General Sean McKeon usually headed the election count in Longford Town. As a matter of fact, I have a double-barrelled shotgun that belonged to him. I had a single barrelled shotgun myself and I swopped it with Bernie Garran who was from Clonbraney in the parish of Kenagh. Bernie was an officer in the Free State Army and he invited me over to shoot in Clonbraney. He gave me a loan of the gun that day and I fell in love with it. I loved going out game shooting and kept it up all my life. Every year I looked forward to the shooting season. As well as that, I loved fishing.

I was transferred from Foighla back to Ferbane around 1947. I was only a short time in Ferbane, about four months. They had a good football team in Ferbane. Years after I met Tony McTeague, the Offaly footballer, in Ferbane. His father had been Sergeant when I was there in 1948. It was a good business town especially on Mondays when the pig fair was on the Main Street. This suited us as a pub was attached to Egan's Grocery. Along with us there were seven pubs in the town. We used to buy corn from the farmers in 20 stone sacks at the railway station. It was sent in by train to Tullamore which was our headquarters. I was acting Manager at that time.

I came back to Clonaslee in 1948 as manager and the manager in Clonaslee, Sean Mooney, was transferred to Ferbane. Little did I know that I was going to spend the rest of my life in Clonaslee - almost 60 years. During those years I have seen many changes. The first big change was the Rural Electrification Scheme, which brought electricity to the town. Many people were afraid of the charges, what would it cost and would they be able to afford it? The electrician who wired the shop was from Tullamore. He came each day on a bicycle. Up to this time the Main Street at night time was always dark. I can remember the switch on of lights the very first night, everybody was out in the street. The local papers had been telling us about it for a while beforehand. It was a wonderful advance at the time. We could now have hot water and do away with the battery radio. It would still be some years before fridges and washing machines came.

Jim Sweeny's wife Maura, with children Frank, Loretta and Donal in the yard behind the shop.

I got married in 1952. My wife was a native of Kilcormac, Maura Dooley. They had a shop in Kilcormac. Father Mahon, a first cousin of my wife, officiated at the wedding ceremony. Maura is dead about twenty years. We had three children, Donal, Loretta and Frank. Donal died in 1999. Times were changing; supermarkets began to appear even though one could say that Egans was a chain of small shops spread over four counties. The two brothers, Pat and Henry Egan, began to close some of the branches that were not viable. They were ageing themselves and really were not up to running the business.

The option came up for some of the managers to buy the business and I did that here in Clonaslee. Egans had other houses on the street and I bought them one by one. I borrowed money from the bank to buy the business and the houses. So Sweeneys now replaced P & H Egan over the shop door. At the same time I began to do a bit of auctioneering. As you can see that is now written over the door:

Auctioneers and Valuers,
James Sweeney M.I.A.V.I.
Tel. 28023

I began to auction houses, farms, and setting of meadows. Property was sold by public auction and private treaty. I remember selling the Rectory out in Bellair for the Church of Ireland to Underwoods, who came here from Kildare.

The most I ever had working in the shop were three along with me. Tom Dunne of Clonabeg started as a young fellow with me. Tom Dunne worked with me from May 1958 to August 1971. He then left and went to New Ireland Insurance. He now lives in Mountmellick. Over the years, many young fellows started off with me and then went on to do something else. We kept the week's takings in a safe in the shop and lodged it each Monday in the Bank of Ireland. They came out each week and rented a room in Joe Conroy's Pub. That was very convenient for us. It was a loss to the village when they ceased operations here. D.E. Williams was our main competitor. They had a shop down in the square where Swans was and later Selma's. Swans rented the premises to D.E. Williams. Swan was a policeman who married into that shop. It was a thatched shop, two-storey, general merchant.

Behind the counter. L-R: Seamus Finlay, Tommy Dunne and Jim Sweeney.

Over the years as business began to change, I thought of getting out of the business. Gradually I closed down as I began to take in less stock. The first thing to go was the grain. I was depending on Egans to take the grain and when they closed down their business it became more difficult. So I began to give more time to the auctioneering. I remember selling a farm out in Coolagh. Then I began to sell houses and sites. This began to take up most of my time. I became a member of the Irish Auctioneers Association. This involved going to Dublin and sitting before a Board of Directors who were mainly trying to find out if I was a suitable person. They asked me questions as to whether I had any experience of selling property and had I anyone who would go guarantor for me. I took out a bond through the Bank, which meant lodging three thousand pounds. They gave me a Certificate stating that I was a fit member of the Association. I still have that Certificate. My son Donal qualified as an auctioneer and continued the business and converted the shop into a supermarket.

Slowly, all the Egan branches closed down. I certainly enjoyed my time with them and was grateful for the opportunity they gave me to get started in life.

Clonaslee was a great little place for fly-fishing. Two little rivers run through the village. I was a member of the Fishing Club. Fr Fleming started the club. We had about sixty members from Clonaslee and district. I was secretary of the

Jim Sweeney hunting with pointer dog.

club for some years. As the rivers gradually got polluted, the club began to dwindle. I fished in Pallas Lake and in the Silver River, Kilcormac. One day I caught a brown trout weighing over two pounds in that river. I'd say that was the biggest catch I ever had.

As a young boy I used to go on holidays to uncles and aunts who lived in Ballyboggin. Not many people in Clonaslee know where Ballyboggin is. It is outside Edenderry in the parish of Ballinabracky and is in Co Westmeath. The postal address was Ballyboggin, Kinnegad. I fished and swam in the River Boyne which runs near my uncle's farm. I still have cousins living there called Williams.

Jerry Bracken

Left Right, Left Right, About Turn

JERRY BRACKEN, CAPPAROGAN

I am an Offaly man. I was born in the parish of Killeigh, Raheen which is between Cloneygowan and Geashill. There was a one-teacher school in Raheen and I was a pupil there for nine years. Mrs Bridget McLoughlin was the teacher. She rode a bike every day, hail, rain or snow from Mountmellick to Raheen, which was about nine miles. She had a car but because it was during the war she could not get petrol. She was a native of County Mayo and her husband was a Guard in Mountmellick. She was a disciplinarian and a very good teacher. Sometimes she had an assistant who looked after the infants. The numbers at the school varied between twenty eight and forty.

I was the eldest of nine and after school I went working on the farm until I was about twenty one years of age. At that time one of the teachers from Portarlington Vocational School, Mr Rattigan, used to come to the local hall where he gave classes twice a week in woodwork. The hall in Cloneygowan was small and was built in 1911. Talking with the other pupils we began to look at the possibility of extending it. The trustees were all dead except Joe Scally who had taken up trusteeship from his father. They had a shop in Cloneygowan and it is now known as Murphy's shop. He was helpful and was all in favour of extending it. The license on the hall had lapsed. We formed a new committee and applied for a renewal of the old license. This was granted by the District Judge at the Court in Portarlington. The Committee of which I was Secretary began fundraising. Looking back we got the money, by today's standards it was not much, but it was difficult to get back then. Mr Molloy from the Co-op in Tullamore was a great help to us. He had been involved in the building of Cappincur Hall. It is now used as an Oratory in the parish of Daingean. We bought all the materials in Tullamore at the Co-op. All the lads after work turned up and we built the extension within a year.

We reformed the local football club. Cloneygowan GAA had a team many years prior to this. They then joined up with Geashill to form St Marys GAA Club. This club went on to win the Offaly County Final around 1950. Local people began to say we should revive our own team again. So Cloneygowan decided to break away from St Marys. It did not cause too much animosity because staying with St Marys involved cycling three to five miles. Training took place on the local green and also in a field provided by Matt Carey. He was the grandfather of Garda Matt Dunne who served in Clonaslee for a number of years.

I became Secretary of the reformed Cloneygowan GAA Club and became very involved in the running of the club. At that time a new Parish Priest, Father Dan Kennedy came to the area. He replaced Father Michael Kennedy who had been very involved in getting Clonsast, Bord na Mona up and running. Father Dan Kennedy had been Administrator in the Cathedral in Carlow and while there was involved in the C.Y.M.S. - Catholic Young Men's Society. On arrival in the parish of Killeigh one of the first things he did was to set up a branch of the C.Y.M.S. He brought Dan Boland, Bernie Connell, myself and one other, whose name escapes me, to a meeting in Carlow to see how the organisation worked. It was their AGM and Bishop Keogh was present. Dan Boland's daughter Bridie Dunne now teaches in Castlecuffe National School. This all happened in 1957. I was elected Secretary of the C.Y.M.S. and it shortly became the umbrella group in the parish for many other activities.

However, my life was about to change direction because on January 24th 1958 I applied to join the Guards. Fifty men from all over Ireland assembled at the Garda Depot in the Phoenix Park to commence our training. It was the first batch of fifty to ever begin training. We lived in Parkgate Hall on Parkgate Street and went up each day for our training. The training officer was Superintendent O'Halloran assisted by Superintendent Patrick Barrett. They had a staff of Sergeants who took charge of various elements of our training. The fifty recruits were divided into two groups for Police duty. This consisted of studying three police manuals, which contained all the procedures relevant to our work as Guards. This was difficult, as we had to sit an exam every four weeks. Our training consisted of how to investigate crime; traffic accidents; the day to day running of a Garda Station; how to treat prisoners; and the handling of records.

At the beginning of our training, drilling on the Depot Square was the priority. Some of us were more awkward than others and each day two hours were given to marching and formation. When we came near to passing out more time was given to marching with the Garda Band in preparation for the display on Graduation Day. Like the Army there was an emphasis on presenting a spic and span image. Uniform, buttons, and footwear had to be shining. Most of our drilling sergeants had been army men and they barked out their orders in no uncertain fashion. One heard in ones sleep *"Left, Right, Left, Right, About Turn, Left Wheel, Right Wheel."*

In those days training was for six months then we were sent out to a Garda Station for a year. We then went back for a refresher course for a month. Part of the month's refresher course was court procedure and accidents. We could now discuss more thoroughly problems we had encountered during our first year.

My first year was spent attached to Harcourt Terrace Station in the B District of Dublin. We wore different letters on our uniforms in different stations in the Dublin Metropolitan Area.

Harcourt Terrace Station had within its area protection posts. For example Government Buildings; the Department of External Affairs; Dail Eireann; museums including the National Gallery. We looked after these on weekends in conjunction with Pearse Street Station. The most important work of all was our stint on duty guarding the British Embassy at 39 Merrion Square. As a matter of fact I was sent over from Mountjoy Station the evening it was attacked and burned in 1969 at the beginning of 'The Troubles'. It was a tough situation as the Embassy was attacked. Stones, bottles and every kind of missile were thrown. I was on the receiving end of a large stone, which hit my chest. We were completely surrounded so one could get out of not going to a hospital.

I spent two and a half years in Harcourt Terrace before moving to Pearse Street. I remained in Pearse Street for seven years from 1961 - 1967.

Pearse Street was considered a tougher area than Harcourt Terrace. The area stretched from the South Docks up to Christ Church Cathedral and across to the top of Grafton Street. The Grand Canal divided us from Ringsend. Harcourt Street was considered a more select area as it had within its confines Stephen's Green, Merrion Square; Fitzwilliam Street, Upper and Lower and Pembroke Street. On the other hand Pearse Street had a lot of flats and the Dock area. In the beginning I specialised in traffic related duty, which included parking and point duty. There were thirty of us assigned to this duty in Pearse Street. De Valera was in residence in Aras an

Sergeant Jerry Bracken on the beat.

Uachtaráin at that time so when diplomats or Ministers from other countries were going to present their credentials traffic had to be held up. When an important Prelate died in a Dublin Hospital his body was brought down Grafton Street on its way to Armagh so he had to get a motor cycle escort up to the border.

In 1963 President Kennedy from the USA visited Ireland. It was a great occasion as it was the first time an American President came to Ireland. Because of his Irish ancestry he took Ireland by storm. It was a very good-humoured event. On his arrival in

- Talking Memories -

Dublin I was stationed at the junction of College Green and Westmoreland Street. He got a great reception as he passed by, standing up and waving to everybody. He looked very young to be President of the United States. During the Patrician Year, Cardinal Agaginian visited Dublin as Papal Legate. Again great crowds appeared on the streets and we in traffic control had extra work on our hands.

During those years Telefis Eireann was inaugurated. On December 31st 1961 there was heavy snow on the ground so I walked down from Rathmines to the Gresham Hotel in O'Connell Street where some of the opening scenes were shot. Gay Byrne hosted the opening along with other luminaries.

Prior to this a notable and sad event had to be patrolled in 1960. The bodies of nine soldiers, who were ambushed on their tour of duty in Namibia, Congo were brought home and given a State Funeral. I was on duty on O'Connell Street as the remains of the young soldiers were brought to Glasnevin Cemetery.

Pearse Street was the busiest Garda Station in the city of Dublin and still is, and because of its proximity to Dublin Castle one bumped into very many of the top brass.

After four years I was taken off Traffic duties, taken into the station at Pearse Street and made assistant to the station Sergeant. His name was Ned Flaherty, a Kerryman and had been my Sergeant on Traffic duties.

My new role was to liaison with the general public and deal with all calls that came into the station. Also, I was put in charge of the duty roster. It was a change and of course I was learning more about the internal workings of the Station.

During 1966, there were celebrations to commemorate the Fiftieth Anniversary of the Easter Rising. Various monuments and plaques were erected throughout the city at junctions where fighting had taken place. A plaque was erected at Boland Mills and these had to be protected by Guards on duty.

- *Talking Memories* -

John Molloy and Jerry Bracken, former colleagues in front of Clonaslee Garda Station.

The following year 1967 I was transferred on promotion to Mountjoy Garda Station. I was to spend the next twelve years there. Prior to leaving Pearse Street I was promoted to Sergeant on August 1st 1967.

Mountjoy Station was not as big an operation as Pearse Street. There were about sixty Guards in Mountjoy while in Pearse Street there were well over a hundred men. It was a big change as one day I was one of the lads and now I was in authority going out inspecting the work being done. In city stations there are usually two or even three Sergeants, each with a unit of twelve to fifteen men. One was an outside Sergeant who was responsible for serious breaches of the law, fatal accidents, fires and anything unusual. The inside Sergeant was the overall supervisor. The first five years of my tenure were spent outside. We were tied in with

the Bridewell and if their station Officer was away we, in
Mountjoy, were responsible for both Bridewell and the running of
our own station. The Mater Hospital was under our jurisdiction.
Weekends were particularly busy and we were constantly under
pressure as fatalities were brought in. This meant that we were
called in to view the body, get identification from relatives, outline
the circumstance of the death and prepare a Coroner's report.
This report had to be done by the following morning.

If the outside Sergeant in the Bridwell was away we were
also responsible for the Richmond Hospital as well, which was in
that area. The Richmond Hospital hadn't as many casualties as the
Mater, but it had a lot of sudden deaths due to head injuries, as it
was well known and specialised in head and brain operations.
Mountjoy became very busy from 1969 as the 'Troubles' in the
North commenced. We became responsible for 'special security'
on the outside wall of Mountjoy prison. Also St Patrick's
Institution for Juveniles, which is surrounded by the same
outward wall, was also under our jurisdiction. One very daring
incident was the helicopter rescue from the Mountjoy prison
courtyard of IRA prisoners. This really put Mountjoy into world
headlines and from then on political prisoners were transferred to
Portlaoise where both Army and Guards were deployed.
Dalymount was also in our area. We were responsible for the
policing of all games there, especially International matches.

On April 3rd 1970, Guard Fallon was shot in a bank raid in
Arran Quay. He was attached to our station in Mountjoy.
Everybody was shocked. This had never happened before and for
days the public were bringing in wreaths to the station. Dick
Fallon was about ten years older than we were and his little boys
were often in the station. So his sudden death had affected us all.
At that time I was the youngest sergeant in Mountjoy and I am
very proud of the fact that two of my unit later became Assistant
Commissioners of the Gardaí.

The funeral of Garda Fallon was a very big occasion. He received a State Funeral from Mount Argus Church to his home parish of Balgriffin, County Dublin. Suddenly we became aware that we were now potential targets as the Northern Ireland struggle became more serious. At the end of that year I was put on inside duties. One of the big changes was that I now could not leave the station for eight and quarter hours. There was a three relieve - as it was called - to cover a twenty four hour period. The quarter hour was to hand over and brief the person coming on duty. Inside you were responsible for prisoners and for the whole running of the station. I was responsible for the remand prisoners in Mountjoy when they had to be brought to a country court. For instance a prisoner might have to be brought up to Donegal in the winter time which meant leaving at 2 am. Escorts had to be provided and arrangements had to be made for transport from the depot.

In May 1974 the Dublin bombings occurred. It was a beautiful sunny day. I happened to be on the roof of Phibsbourgh Shopping Centre when I heard a loud thud. On getting home I heard what had happened. I went to the station and from there to the Mater Hospital where a lot of the casualties had been brought. It was mayhem. People were injured, people dead, relatives coming to inquire as word spread around the city. As people did not return home more relatives came to the Mater seeking information. Over the next week I was constantly down to the Mater Hospital while the working day at the station had to continue as normal.

In 1979 I was transferred as Sergeant to Clonaslee. Clonaslee had become vacant with the transfer of Sergeant Doherty to Monivea, County Galway. I knew of Clonaslee as it was only sixteen miles from my native place. At that time there were four guards and a Sergeant stationed in Clonaslee. This was because our duties involved supplying one man daily to Portlaoise

Prison. Another man would be seconded for a month's duty at the prison. This was known as temporary transfer. While I, myself had to go in three times a week and also do a month three times a year. We lived first in Bonastick renting a house from Tom and Pauline Horan who made us feel very welcome. They had two little ponies, Pepper and Flipper. Our children fell in love with them and this made their transition down the country much easier.

We came on September 3rd 1979 and our children transferred from Dublin Schools to the local schools. Colum, our eldest, began the Leaving Certificate year in St Mary's College, Mountmellick, which he enjoyed very much. The other four commenced in the Vocational School and the local primary school.

I settled in quickly finding the people more than friendly. I understood the people from my own upbringing and I found the people up the mountain very welcoming.

In relation to my work I was dealing directly with the public, whereas in Mountjoy I had a big staff and so would not have been dealing with everything personally. I had no great night duty except when I went into the prison. When they began to reduce the number of men in the prison Clonaslee lost some of its guards as well. Through my work as Sergeant I became involved in local affairs especially Muintir na Tire and the Community Council. Eventually I became Chairman of the Community Council. Every year I represented the local branch of Muintir along with others at their annual convention. I remember going to Athlone, Nenagh, Limerick, Gort and Cork. Several were held in Tipperary Town because of its association with the late Canon Hayes, founder of Muintir na Tire.

The GAA Club, St Manmans nominated me to be their treasurer. I held that post for ten to twelve years. I enjoyed being involved in local affairs, as it helped people know me as well as I getting to know them.

I was Sergeant in Clonaslee for twelve years, retiring in

1991. I enjoyed my time here as Sergeant receiving great co-operation from the community.

The family in May 1972. Back L-R: Jo & Jerry Bracken, Diarmaid.
Front L-R: Colum, Patricia, Enda and Ann.

When we came here the Village Green was a wild grassy area. Bonfires were lit when a local team won. Today it is well kept with a lovely lawn kept by John O'Keeffe, flowers and shrubs and is a lovely entrance to the village from the Birr Road. There were no Christmas lights then and through the efforts of the Community Council and Tidy Towns our village has become a lovely place to live.

I met my wife in 1959 through an accident which I was sent to investigate. A girl called Jo Egan was cycling to work in Pearse Street Library when she was struck by a double decker bus, No 20. It was the day of a Presidential election, June 17th 1959. I went to take a statement in the Meath Hospital as the accident had occurred at the top of Harcourt Street and Harcourt Road, which was in our Garda area. There was a court case later on in the year, in August, and our paths crossed again as I had to present the case and Jo had to give evidence. This led to our marriage in 1961.

Alice Kennedy

From Shracullen to Oxford Street

ALICE KENNEDY, SHRACULLEN

I was born in Brocca near to where Tom Higgins lived. When I was six months old my family moved up to Shracullen. My brother Chris now lives there. Also living here in the area are my sisters Kit and Mary Anne while my brother Michael lives at the top of the hill. We all went to school in Clonaslee walking across the fields. At the time they belonged to Bill Furlong. There was a Mass Path across the fields. It is now grown over. It came out at the shop called The Store. It was run by

John Cusack, of Tullamore Co-op, the father of Evelyn who is a presenter on R.T.E. The ruins of the shop were there up to recently. The Gorrough River and Bridge is close by.

After primary school I went to the Technical School which is now closed since its relocation. I worked in Cusack's for a few years before moving to Salts in Tullamore. A bus used to come to Clonaslee and it gave good employment in the area. A man called Mr Greene was in charge. We were all afraid of him. We regarded him as a tyrant. You were made aware when he was coming as he shouted a lot. It was a woollen mills so the name Salts does not seem to fill the bill. Girls came to work there from all the neighbouring towns and villages. At any given time there were around two to three hundred employed. The wool came on large spools and our job was to wind it down on to smaller spools. It was then sent to England where Salts had another factory in the North. There were two shifts; one in the morning from 8 am to 3 pm and the other one was from 3 pm to 10 pm. I preferred the later shift as we did not have to get up that early and we had more fun. The building is still there on the left as you go down to the Railway Station.

There was a camogie team in Clonaslee trained by Mamie Poole and Mick Maher, Eilish Maher's husband. Mamie Poole was a camogie player herself. She knew all the rules, got a few of us girls together and brought us up to the hurling field in Brittas to train. One girl brought another and we entered the local championships. Our uniform was wine colour pinafore with a white blouse, black socks and plimsolls - canvas shoes. Mamie Poole provided us with the hurleys and hurling balls. If a hurley broke she had spare ones under her arm going up and down the side-line. Mick Maher was on the other side shouting instructions and encouragement. Jack Dunne also helped. We reached the final the first year against Mountmellick. It was played in Ballylinan. The team went by cars while a big following went by bus.

Before the final was played I had gone to England to be bridesmaid at my brother Michael's wedding. This wedding took place in Widnes, Lancashire. When I was at the wedding I decided I would stay on and look for work. This was August 1962. I got word from Clonaslee pleading for me to come back and play the final. They obviously felt I would be an asset to the team. I came by boat from Liverpool to Dublin and got the train to Tullamore. I arrived on the Friday before the match. I usually played left corner back alongside Mary McCann, now married to Brian Callaghan. We were losing the match when Jack Dunne, Tom Kearney and Mamie Poole had a conference on the side-line and changes were made. I ended up playing full back. The whole game changed. Joe Young reminds me often that things got tense and tougher on the field and that I had words with Lily Kirwan, the Mountmellick full forward - that is putting it mildly!

Alice Kennedy on an outing to Athlone in 1960

We won the game. Mountmellick had two teams and felt they would have no trouble beating Clonaslee in the first game. They were very disappointed. I was carried off shoulder high and have great memories of that day. There were no cameras at that time so I have no photograph of the event.

- Talking Memories -

I can remember Mesa Bates, Kit Fitzgerald, Ann Dunne, Marie Rosney playing on the team. I cannot remember the other players. I went back to England on the Monday bringing the medal with me. I still have it in London. As there was no camogie team in England this was my last game.

In the same month of September, I moved to London, Kentish Town, where I stayed in the same house as my brother Joe Culliton. Mary Digan of Coolagh, Joe Digan's sister, also stayed in the same house. The two of us had gone away together. I went to work in Woolworth's. It was a famous London store then with branches all over. They had a well-known branch in Dublin. I think they were located in Henry Street. They were also in Cork and Belfast. I was seven and a half years working there as a shop assistant and then promoted to supervisor. I enjoyed working there, got on well with the staff and management and met many Irish people each day as they came in to shop.

Alice Kennedy among the roses.

After almost a decade I decided to move and went to work in a department store, John Lewis' on Oxford Street, not far from Piccadilly Centre. Oxford Street is a worldwide famous shopping street in the West End of London. I began working as a cashier in the electrical department. They sold everything; clothes, furniture, hardware, carpets. I then became service clerk dealing with electrical complaints. I found the change easy and loved every minute of it. It meant that if any mechanical purchase broke down from toasters to kettles to washing machines to fridges, I sent out engineers to the house and followed up on the complaint. It is a very large department store, five stories high with over two thousand people working there. Despite the present recession it is still doing very well.

I worked there for thirty two and a half years. I went in by bus every day, No 3 or 53, and the last four years I walked to work every day through Regents Park. Regents Park is a beautiful park in the centre of London. The London Zoo is located there. It took me fifty five minutes to walk in from door to door so it was a way of keeping fit. The flowers are lovely in the park all colours and shades. The company always knew I would be in on time and present, especially if there was ever a bus or underground strike.

John Lewis Store is an unusual store because it is a Partner Store. Each employee is considered to be an integral partner in the store. This in practice meant that each year, at the end of March, when the financial state of the company was announced each employee shared in the profits. This meant that any percentage of profit was shared in the wages you were receiving. So in the first week of April each year a lump sum of cash was paid to each employee. In my thirty two years this varied from sixteen per cent to twenty four per cent. Naturally the day of the bonus announcement was a great day. A few of us from the shop floor would go up to the staff dining room where we would meet the chairman of John Lewis. One member of the staff would be given an envelope which contained a letter detailing the percentage of bonus that year. Back we would go to our departments - most of the time happy with the outcome. A few years the bonus was low depending on that year's profits. This encouraged staff to stay longer and look after our customers better. At Christmas there was always a Christmas dinner. There were three sittings as there was up to two thousand staff. The managers all served the dinner. The first sitting at 11.30 am then 12.30 pm and the final sitting at 1.30 pm. It was always very enjoyable with a great atmosphere.

After twenty five years one got six months holidays and sabbatical leave. One's money went into the bank as usual. There was great camaradarie among the staff. We would often go out together in the evenings. Each department also arranged their own social evenings in pubs around the West End. When I went there first the manufacturers would also take us out to make sure we would promote their goods. They always took us to a posh restaurant where we would get the best of everything. The company was very good to their staff.

At the end of my thirty two and a half years I was not feeling that well however if I retired I would lose a certain amount of my pension. So the company said I could retire because I was so good to them and they would be good to me and they decided they would pay me full wages for the next two years and then give me my entitlements along with quite a good lump sum tax free. When I was sixty five they brought me back in for my retirement party - which they did for all employees. They facilitated me when my mother was sick and allowed me home for a long spell, full pay, to be with her. When I went back they called me in and gave me a week's holidays as they said I needed it. I still go back to see some of my former colleagues but many have retired like myself. Of course the store has been completely re-vamped and I have been told conditions of work have changed. It is not the same as in my day. It was a marvellous place to work, one big happy family.

Alice Kennedy in front of John Lewis Department Store in Oxford Street.

During the "Troubles" there was a bomb scare. We were all evacuated quickly and we all went down to Christies, the famous auctioneers where we were all given refreshments and allowed to make phone calls. In the afternoon we all went back. A small device had been found in the toilets and made safe. This occurrence made big news back home in Ireland. After this, every morning when we went in and each evening before we left each person had to check their own section.

I met my husband Frank during those years when I was in John Lewis. We were happily married for eighteen years. He was a Tipperary man from Lorrha on the Offaly border. I met him at a friend's house. In 2002 I retired from John Lewis, which is when my life started. This was to be the fun part of my life when I ceased working and became an active volunteer in many organisations.

I became very involved in our local church, St Dominic's Priory, Southampton Road. First of all I went on the Parish Council. Then I went on the Financial Council. I then began to organise the cleaners which is once a week. Jumble sales were held once a month. My experience in John Lewis being much appreciated. The Jumble sales were always great fun. I am one of the collectors each Sunday morning at 8.30 am mass and the next day Monday I help count the money. The Ministry of the Eucharist plays a big part in my life as I bring communion to the sick in the parish. It is a big parish and our church, which is one hundred and forty years old, could be described as a small cathedral. It can hold about five hundred and fifty people. There are ten to twelve priests in the parish, all Dominican. Some of them teach, others are chaplains to hospitals and schools and they range in age from eighty downwards.

When I retired I was approached to join the Irish Pensioners Club. They came looking for me as they needed a Secretary. At present the Chairperson is unable to do any work and so I find myself acting as Chairperson, Secretary and Treasurer. We meet in Tower Block on the nineteenth floor every Thursday afternoon. There are about thirty members. We are sponsored by the Irish Government as most of our members are Irish. Due to the economic recession at the moment our sponsorship has gone down. We organise outings - mostly seaside to Eastbourne, Southend and Clacton. Some of our members don't see many people. They live in the sheltered Tower Block where there are ninety flats. This weekly 'get together' is important. If they are missing I ring them up and check on them.

A lady called Sally Mullready, who is a counsellor in Hackney has been invited to go on the President Michael D. Higgins Committee. She got in touch with me about forming a choir of older Irish people. She wanted to keep the Irish songs alive in England. We produced a CD called *Love and Emigration* which was launched in September 2011. We rehearsed in the Irish Centre, Camden Town every Monday for two years. Sally does a lot for older Irish people, such as getting benefits and their Irish pension.

- *Talking Memories* -

Irish Pensioners Choir at Theatro Technis in Camdem April 2012.
Alice Kennedy is front row second from left.

The CD was a great success. It sold a thousand copies. We sang in the House of Commons. We were the backing group for Tommy Fleming, when he sang *'Hard Times'* in Trafalgar Square at the St Patrick's Day parade. We also visit many nursing or care homes where we sing for the residents. We have a small drama group in the choir where we put on plays. We did excerpts from *'Juno and the Paycock'* by Sean O'Casey and *'The Merry Widow'*.

The Irish Elderly Advice Network was set up in 1997. It has twelve trustees and I am the chairperson. They have an office in Camden Town. It was set up after two Irishmen were found dead in their flats. At the time people were not as conscientious as now, two Irish ladies, Margaret Byrne and Bridie McGowan, saw the need and set it up. They are still trustees. I am down there most days. As Chairperson the work is there to be done. Three people are there all the time. Sally Mullready is the main person with all the knowledge. The Network is sponsored by the Irish Government and the Ireland Fund for Great Britain and Camdon Council and Bridge House. They look after Irish people all over London, helping them with their problems.

Alice Kennedy and Una Purcy with Dermot Aherne, Minister of Foreign Affairs
at the Irish Embassy

I love coming home to visit my family - my sisters, brothers and relations. My sister Kit was one time Secretary of the I.C.A. She was very involved in all competitions. She acted on the stage and was a real comedian. She and my sister Mary Anne were involved in the Clonaslee Show looking after the entries. Competitions attracted a lot of competitors who had to be taken care of. Kit and the President took care of the annual outing on June 29th. Mrs Frank Dunne was also very involved and always organised a dance on the way home. There was a great social in the old Vocational School every year. The supper was the main attraction and young people were never refused.

Eamon Sammon

Green Keeper

EAMON SAMMON, COOLAGH

At present one family, Bernard and Helen Multaney along with their boy Brian, live on our lane in Coolagh. It was also known as *"The Farm"*. I don't know where this name came from. Some say there was a farmer with three daughters who lived here years ago. He divided the farm among his daughters so giving the locality its name "The Farm". One time there were five families living here. Now there are only the Multaneys and the Sammons.

I went to school in Castlecuffe. Josie Daly brought me to

school on my first day. I remember it well. She brought me through Behans across fields to the school. It was a short cut to the main road. Behans lived beside the school. Kevin O'Leary now lives there. It was a one room school; the room looked very long and big to me. All the seven classes were in the one room. There was a long stool across the middle. That was the partition. On one side were Infants, First and Second class. On the other side was Third, Fourth, Fifth and Sixth class. I started in the school just before the summer holidays. The Principal was Mrs Twomey. She lived in Clonaslee where Dr Sheehan lives now and she herself was married to a doctor. He was dead at that time. Her three children, Bill, Paddy and Anne were pupils in the school. They came every day to school accompanying their mother in her car. It was a green Baby Ford. There were only two other cars in Clonaslee, Jimmy Dunne and Bill Brien. Father Doyle had a bicycle and used to visit the school. I can't remember the other teacher.

Mrs Redmond taught me in First Class, Miss Carmel Nolan, who was known as a J.A.M. Junior Assistant Mistress, also taught me. A J.A.M. is a teacher who isn't fully qualified but is still allowed to teach. After several years the Department of Education brought in a six week course over two successive summers to bring them up to full teachers. This post is no longer in existence. I then had Mrs Twomey who was replaced by Mr Tom Honan. He was a native of

Eamon Sammon as a young boy

Clare. Carmel Nolan came from Baltinglass. There were between fifty and sixty pupils going to the school. I can remember meeting Jim Multaney in the school. He was three classes ahead of me and we have been good neighbours all over the years since then. Annie Salmon, who lived beside our house, was related to Jim. As you can see she spelled her surname different to me. That was supposed to be the fish. I suppose if one went back in the Register you would come across an 'L' instead of the second 'M'. That is only speculation of course.

Tom Honan and Carmel Nolan took a leading part in the local dramatic group. They both moved on to Arklow and were replaced by Stasia McRedmond and Mr Daffy. I think Mr Kelly then became Principal. I found school hard. The building was very old. The windows were in bad repair. The floorboards had holes in them. It looked a solid building with the one door - the main door - on the east side of the school facing Clonaslee. At that time there was no running water. For the nine years I was there I came across the fields and went home across the fields each day. In the final year I sat the Primary Certificate. It was held in the Girls School in Clonaslee. I could never find the Certificate. I know I got it and it would be nice if I could find it. This school was demolished and a new school was built in 1953. It has since been extended and an acre of ground is being purchased at the back to provide more playing facilities. There are now three full time teachers with children coming from the local area and from Clonaslee. There have been great changes since my time.

My first job was with the E.S.B. I started on August 14th 1962 in Pooles Field. I spent three years there. The work was hard. It involved digging holes, hoisting poles and then climbing the pole to bind in the wire which carried the electricity. One had to have a good head for heights. All of those working with me were local men. The wages were seven pounds and one shilling. The day began at 8.15 am and ended at 5.30 pm. Everyone arrived by bicycle. I bought a Raleigh bike in Lanterys of Cadamstown. I still have the bicycle and it cost sixteen pounds. It was an ordinary Raleigh bike with a dynamo, which is the name of the light put on the front of the bike. It was like a new car to me. The E.S.B. worked mostly around Clonaslee though I do remember spending a week in Kilkenny doing the same work in heavy snow. We stayed down there for the week.

That work finished up and I moved to the Forestry. Work was scarce in those days much like now. A lot of the work was up in Glendine and around the Cut. We planted up there. It has since been cut and planted again. The Forestry gave good employment and after three years the single men were let off as work began to slacken. After three years I moved back to the E.S.B. and worked from their base in Monasterevan. This work took me all over County Kildare so I got to know the county well. I drove what is known as a stringing machine which was located on the back of a lorry. The wire was released from the machine by pulling it to where it was needed. And so another three years passed. I went back and forth to the E.S.B. several times afterwards. Clonaslee men were highly thought of in the E.S.B. Sean Conroy from Durrow, County Laois always held Clonaslee men in high regard and would always take them on whenever possible.

In 1970 I moved to the Golf Club in Tullamore where I was to spend the next twenty years. Jim Multaney told me about the job, as he knew about it from John Flanagan, who later built the Court Hotel and many other buildings including schools in Tullamore. The first job I had to do was to install a sprinkling system for the greens. I then became grounds man in the Club. It was all walking then, no golf buggies or other modern equipment. The Golf Club had a big membership then which included Mrs Kitty McCann who became the first Irish woman to win the British Amateur Open. She was a magnificent golfer. Kitty had a wonderful long drive and could hold her own with the men. She was also great around the greens especially in chipping and putting. She spent many hours practising. I saw a lot of golf, good and bad.

Raking the bunker, Eamon Sammon

My main work was taking charge of the greens. As green keeper, the greens had to be mowed every day in the summer time. I used a cylinder mower up and down and they had to be cut at a different angle every day. On the week of the Captain's Prize a lot of extra work had to be taken on. That week involved an early start. This pattern followed in many competitions throughout the year. There were a few scratch players in the Club at that time, Dinny White, Sean Flanagan, Sean Larkin who also worked on the course and Liam Adams. During tournaments I was also always present in case of an emergency. I can remember Christy O'Connor Junior coming to the Club and playing an exhibition match. I enjoyed the work there. It was all outdoors and kept me very fit as I walked miles over the course each day.

During the winter, part of my work was preparing temporary greens for the players as the permanent greens needed to be repaired. This involved sanding, putting on compost and manure to keep the greens healthy. The greens are considered to be the most important part of the club. Some are fast, some slow. The club would be judged on the condition of the greens.

Eamon Sammon, on the green

After twenty enjoyable years at the club I moved to the Midland Health Board. There I drove a Day Care Bus for sixteen years. My run was Clonaslee on a Monday; Ballyfin on a Tuesday; Portarlington on a Wednesday; Clonaslee/Rosenallis on Thursday and Mountmellick on Friday.

Each day I brought different people to the Day Care Centres. Most of them were old, one person whom I brought twice a week from Rosenallis to Mountmellick Day Care Centre, Mrs Byrne, died one month short of her hundredth birthday. We had all been invited to her birthday party on St Stephen's Day but unfortunately it was not to be.

A book was recently published, *"Ireland's Wild Orchids - a Field Guide"* by Brendan Sayers and Susan Sex. Orchids can be found in a variety of habitats in Ireland. The North Bull Island in

Dublin is home to eight orchid species and their hybrids.

The book is a beautiful presentation with wonderful photographs by Leveen Hill and Jackie O'Connell. Strange as it may seem to all my neighbours, Jackie O'Connell, who is a retired priest of our diocese, Kildare and Leighlin, has been coming here for many years to take photographs of a rare orchid which grows at the back of the sandpit which is near my house in Coolagh. The first time he came here Father Shortall, then Parish Priest of Clonaslee, accompanied him. They were classmates in Maynooth Seminary. In the month of June the road into my house is covered with orchids. All around the sandpit is a mass of pink.

I was always fascinated by the length of time it took to get the proper photograph. Father O'Connell would lie flat down on the ground for hours shooting from various angles, close-ups, all the while waiting for a cloud to disappear so that he had the correct sunlight. If a shower came, everything would stop.

I also know that he spent time each year in Cush Bog where more orchids are to be found. He would say to me, *"Tomorrow I must visit Lough Annagh"*, formerly a lake but now drained, down where McCanns live.

The Fly Orchid found at the sandpit on Eamon Sammon's land.

The habitat of a rare snail is to be found on the road past the sandpit. The snail is half the size of the nail on your little finger. It is a preserved species. Years back there was a conflict of interest when the bypass at Newbridge, Co Kildare was held up because of a rare snail. The snail was found at Pollardstown Fen.

It was felt that the location of the bypass was too close to the Fen and so would disturb the habitat of the snail.

The three musketeers outside Castlecuffe National School reminiscing about the old school days. L-R: Paddy Delaney, Jim Multaney and Eamon Sammon.

One Saturday five years ago, I began to clean a drain at the side of the road where the snails can be found. A man came from the Environmental Impact Assessment Agency on the following Monday morning to say I would have to fill back the drain as I was disturbing the snails. So I put back in the sods I had removed. How he knew this in the space of two days I will never know. I cannot put cattle out there now. I used to put them there over the winter. It was a great place to winter cattle as you had the dry hills and sandpit. These snails are a rare species and have to be protected.

A similar occurrence is now taking place in regards to turf cutting. Five years ago I received a letter stating that no turf could be cut on my stretch of bog without permission from the relevant Minister. We can still cut with permission. A letter comes each year informing me that I can apply to the Minister seeking permission to cut. So far permission has been granted. However it seems that the bog will shortly be closed and no more turf will be harvested. Our family has been cutting turf here for hundreds of years so it will be a big change.

There have been many changes over the years and I am glad to have lived through them and reached three score and ten.

Sean Ricketts

The Lone Piper

SEAN RICKETTS, BROCCA

I began playing the bag pipes when I was sixteen years of age. My mother was a great melodeon player. Our house was a great ceili house. People were always calling to play and sing songs at night time. Our kitchen was next to the road beside what was known as the Metal Bridge. Bord na Mona called the new one, Ricketts Bridge. The Board of Works came regularly to read the depth of the water.

The first musical instrument I learnt to play was the mouth

organ. I then learned to manage the tin whistle. I saw neighbours Paddy Kane and Shud Conroy playing them so I went off and bought one in Clarkes of Tullamore. Paddy Kane lived on Chapel Street next to where the new houses are now. My mother died when I was thirteen years old. She was a good melodeon player and I can remember people saying *"Go on Margaret Mary play another one"*. The melodeon was a big one known as the 'Chary' and had four stoppers. Those stoppers were used to change the tone. I had three sisters; Bridie, Ellen and Gret. My only brother, the youngest of us all, was called Jim. Gret, my youngest sister was able to play the accordion. Gret married Jim McCann of Clonabeg and she died recently. Jim, who was nine years younger than me also played the accordion and played in England with a ceili band. He is still alive and lives in London. His health is not good and he is unable to come home any more. He has two sons John and James.

The five of us went to school in Clonaslee. The school was then in Chapel Street. John Bates and Mrs Dunne were the teachers. All the Flynns, Caseys, Dowlings, Coffeys along with the Conroys, Farrells, Saddlers and Hylands went in to Clonaslee School. The metal bridge was the meeting place. In the evenings we played hurling in Condron's field. Mary Condron, when she saw us, would come down and hunt us out of the field.

Everybody in Clonaslee would say to us *"Don't you live near the metal bridge?"* Everything happened and was discussed at the metal bridge. It was our social centre. Skittles was a popular game at the time. Pitch and Toss was often played. On Sunday evenings there would often be a 'session' going into the night time. We were put to bed and so we listened to it until we fell asleep.

I can remember well the first time I heard the Clonaslee Pipe Band playing at the church gates. There was a big crowd and I couldn't even see them but I could hear them through the crowd.

I was about seven years old. I was born in July 1922 so it must have been around 1929 when I first heard them. The old band broke up and I remember Father Doyle calling out in the church that there would be a meeting in the hall to reform the band. This must have been around 1938. After two years I joined the band.

L-R: Paddy McRedmond, Pat Gorman and Sean Ricketts with the Ford Prefect.

I was up in Jim Carroll's house in Coolaboughlan one evening when I was about sixteen. He showed me a practise chanter and gave me the music scales and also the notes of a tune. From there on I went on my own using a practise chanter that Frank Dunne gave me. He was married to Mrs Dunne, the teacher. I kept practising on that one. Several other people, about ten maybe learned off my chanter until I got a new one. I graduated from playing the practise chanter to playing the bag pipes. I went to the hall at night time to watch the band practising. I got the loan of the pipes and brought them home. One night later, in the hall, when the band had a rest I took up one of the pipes and tried to play. I managed to play some way or another, a couple of tunes which I had learned at home. The committee were all present and said *"That's a good start"* and I went on with them and joined up.

My brother Jim, when he saw me learning to play the practise chanter asked if he could learn to play too. So at seven years of age he began to play it and at around eleven years of age, he began to play the pipes in the school.

Frank Dunne lived on Chapel Street. His wife was the local teacher. I think she taught in Killurin before she came to Clonaslee. She was a native of Carlow. His claim to fame - as well as reforming the pipe band in my time, along with Father Doyle, the local curate - was that his sons were to become household names throughout the country in later years. His son Michael became the GAA correspondent with the Irish Press and later with RTE. His son Frank, after studying in Knockbeg College, went to London where he became a well-known actor.

Michael's daughter Eileen is one of the newsreaders on RTE. My father and Frank Dunne were on different committees in the parish. So Frank was a frequent visitor to our house. He was in and out discussing and planning various activities. He was one of the people who encouraged me to take up the pipes.

At night time in the hall he wrote up the notes on the blackboard of different tunes. We played them on the practise chanter. Then he'd say, *"Get the pipes"*. He would turn the blackboard around to see if we had got the tune and notes into our heads. If we made a mistake he corrected us but there was always one who would deliberately play a wrong note in order to get him going. We rehearsed two nights a week depending on who wanted to rent the hall. It was a hive of activity in those days. People played cards, billiards and snooker. The local library was housed there and people came on Sunday to rent books. Films came later on. Dances were held now and again. Different visiting drama groups would include Clonaslee, as they travelled around the country staging different plays. Travelling shows also came and set up on the green itself. Each show set up their own hall. I remember one show called Maccaroni, they were Italian. They had acrobats as well as films. It was a sad day when we heard that their hall had been burnt out in Geashill.

Clonaslee Pipe Band. Back L-R: Tom McCann, Michael Lawlor, Jack Dunne, Mick Dunne, Ned Conroy, Joe Dunne, Mick Kennedy, Sean Ricketts. Front sitting down: Jim Brien.

What was known as the old Pipe Band began in 1910. I remember some of them; from Chapel Street there was Frank Dunne and his brother Joe. Joe later trained Clara Band. Also Hugh Mahon, Tom and Joe Morris, Shuddy Conroy and his brothers, Johnny Dunne from Tinnahinch, Mick Kennedy of Cloonagh Mor and Tom McCann of Cush - I have his pipes.

I must have joined the band around 1940 during the Second World War. Most of them were older than me; Jim Carroll and Dick, Mick Dunne of Broughla and Jack Dunne of Capparogan, Mick Lalor who later became County Chairman of the Laois GAA Hurling Board, Ned Conroy of Graiguefulla, Bernie Conroy from up the mountain.

When I joined there were about ten members. We rehearsed twice a week going over some of the tunes and having a chat. Not all would turn up as some were away working maybe thirty miles away. Frank Dunne was our teacher. Joe Dunne was our staff man. The Pipe Major was Mick Lalor. The colour of our kilt was green and yellow. The tunic being green, the skirt yellow, the stockings green, the shawl yellow and blue caps. The band couldn't afford special shoes - we used our own black shoes. Neither could we afford the spur which was usually tied with a belt. Nor could we afford the Tara Brooch.

We received many invitations to play. Most Sundays throughout the summer we performed at local sport meetings, GAA matches, at opening ceremonies, Christmas Day, New Year's Day, Patrick's Day and Easter Sunday. We would usually march down the village from the hall to the Church of Ireland. We turned there coming back up Main Street, down Chapel Street where we turned and came back up to the hall. The children always loved to follow us. On New Year's Eve we marched down the village at 12 o'clock to play the New Year in. All the people were at their doors clapping, shouting, waving to us as the New Year was welcomed. The children usually went ahead of us and behind us carrying torches lit with sods of turf and paraffin oil. You would be arrested if you went out like that now. There was no electricity then.

One of my first memories was playing at the Aeríocht

which was held in Brady's field beyond what is now known as the sand trap on the Tullamore Road at Brocca. A whole lot of lorries parked for step dancing and music. Local teams played in a hurling tournament for which medals were presented.

This band parted company around 1950. There was a falling out and a disagreement among the members. It reminds me of Brendan Behan's famous remark when, on being asked to chair a meeting, he said to the assembled people, we will now have the first proposal *"I propose a split"*.

Some of the committee were not too happy with me as I did not take sides. Father Doyle came to see me and said *"You don't stir"*. Father Doyle was the Chairman and the band was reformed. I played with them. The band continued with some of the members going somewhere else.

Father P.J. Clear home on holidays from Brazil alongside Sean Ricketts.
Pictures on back wall: Grandfather John Connolly and mother Margaret Mary Connolly.

After two years I got an invitation to join Mount Bolus Pipe Band. Jim, my brother went down the night before to see what the set up was. He liked what he saw. Frank Dunne brought me down to Mount Bolus. In we went, Frank asked me to listen to the Mount Bolus crowd and asked me what I thought of them. I thought they were very good so I joined them. I continued with them as well as playing for Tullamore.

Some of the invitations and performances stand out more than others. The night Offaly won their hurling All Ireland was a special one. We met the Offaly team half a mile outside of Birr and played them into the Square. Thousands of people came to welcome them home. They had already been to Tullamore, the county town, but Birr was always regarded as the capital of the hurling area within the county. It was spilling rain but it cleared away when we arrived in the Square. A platform was erected in front of Dooley's Hotel. We were joined in the square by an accordion band. There were plenty of speeches. It went on right through the night. We played at regular intervals winding up at about 6 am. We made our way home stopping to drink "milk" in Kilcormac.

If there ever was a big day in Tullamore we were always invited. On looking back I have to say it was great to be a member of the three Pipe Bands - Clonaslee, Mount Bolus and Tullamore. I made many friends over the years at various events and I would not have had the opportunity to travel to these places were it not for playing the pipes. People often say you must need great lung power to play the pipes but not when you have practised and put in the work. I often played for a whole hour and was never in any way tired. We always travelled together, three or four in a car. So over the years many friendships were formed. When we met, the first topic was always music. I think it's a big loss to Clonaslee not to have its own band anymore. Everybody loves to see a band marching. It brings great excitement and exhilaration when a band appears. The children love it and feel they are part of it as they march alongside you on the footpaths.

Close by where I live is Father Graham's Well. People, after paying a visit tie ribbons on to the tree at the well and leave medals and beads. One of the stories according to Tom Higgins is that a woman suffering badly from toothache came to the well. Father Graham bathed the water on her face and said *"Them that pray for me, many will be cured here"*.

My grandfather never had a toothache. Over the years local people have had great faith in the well with people from Killoughey, Killurin, Rhode and many other places visiting.

I spent all my life around the metal bridge. It is no longer in use as there is a new one constructed beside it. I have very happy memories of it. I used to go out to the bridge, play the pipes and the Clodiagh River carried the sound and it was heard for miles around. I was affectionately known as the Lone Piper.

I would have preferred if they had kept the metal bridge. It had more character. In 1945 they took down the side pieces. It didn't look the

Sean Ricketts playing the pipes at home.

same. The Board of Works put up a machine on the wall. It is solar powered. It is under the metal bridge. They come every so often to measure the water in the event of a flood.

There was a lake here nearby. Half of it was in Offaly and half in Laois. It was known as Lough Annagh. It was drained in 1952 by the Board of Works. It had many fish; trench, perch, pike and eels. Swans and wild geese flew in every year and they still continue to come. They had water enough in the winter but when Bord na Mona came near it they left. With the drains being cut they had less bog berries.

Mairead Corbet

The War is on Folks

MAIREAD CORBET, BALLYKANEEN

I was born in Johnstown, Co Kilkenny in 1923. My father was a native of Ferrybank in Co Waterford. He was a Primary Teacher and his father before him was also a teacher in Ferrybank. His first teaching post was in Johnstown and he later became Principal in Crosspatrick School in the same parish of Johnstown. It was known locally - as Gaelige - Cros Phádraig. I always said I wouldn't be a Primary Teacher. The fact that I had to go out to Crosspatrick every morning as my father and mother both taught there put me off. My father never drove a car so I cycled out the three miles to the school each day along with them. My father was trained in De La Salle in Waterford which was a Teaching Training College. My mother came from Callan in Co Kilkenny. She was a J.A.M.; Junior Assistant Mistress. She taught Infants, First and Second Class while my father took the senior classes Fifth and Sixth.

In our house Irish was the spoken language. My father and mother had a great love of the Irish language and were of the opinion that you did not have to be living in the Gaeltacht to be able to speak it. Looking back, we were the only family in Johnstown who I think spoke Irish on a daily basis. I can't remember whether Irish was spoken in Johnstown School but it was in Crosspatrick. So I had two languages without being aware of having them. If I were born in Switzerland I would have had two or three languages, as there it is the norm.

Our family went to Ring in County Waterford every summer for our holidays. My father's brother and his family also went to Ring each year. He was a teacher in Ferrybank. There were twelve in his family - there is only one of them left, Joseph - while I was the only one in our family. All my cousins spoke Irish so it was the normal, easy thing to do. The Irish spoken in Ring would have different pronunciation from Connacht and Kerry and completely different from Donegal and Ulster Irish.

From Crosspatrick School I went to the Ursuline Convent School in Thurles where I spent two years. I loved being in Thurles. I was happy there and enjoyed the company of the other girls. I found the Ursuline nuns to be very good teachers. My son Raymond lives in Holycross and his three girls also went to school in Thurles with the Ursulines.

At that time I was interested in Home Economics. My first cousin Sheila Foley had been trained in St Catherine's, Sion Hill, Blackrock so because of that I moved from Thurles to Sion Hill.

While I missed Thurles I got to like Sion Hill. It is out beside Blackrock College. In Sion Hill I spent two years as a boarder. I did my Leaving Certificate there in 1941. In my third year I started my Home Economics Course. As I did not get into teaching I spent a further year in Eccles Street. From there I was called to Cathal Brugha Street. While there I stayed in a hostel at the corner of Gardiner Street and Mountjoy Square. There were twenty-four in my class. We were divided into two groups of twelve. The Irish teacher on the course was Andrias Ó Muineacán who also featured from time to time on Radio Eireann. I spent three years in training in Coláiste Mhuire where I qualified in 1946 as a Domestic Economy Teacher or Home Economics Teacher, as they say now.

The day I went to Dublin to Sion Hill was September 1st 1939. On the way up to Dublin the bus stopped in Naas to take on passengers. The conductor had to leave off papers and when he got back on the bus he announced *'The war is on folks'.*

I learned that Germany bombed Warsaw on that day and England declared war on the 3rd of September. The All-Ireland Hurling Final was then always held on the first Sunday in September. My parents went to the final as Kilkenny was playing Cork. Kilkenny won that day so it was a joyful day. Instead of going to the match I went to the pictures with my two cousins in Manor Street near Aughrim Street, I think.

It was during the Second World War so we had to bring our ration books for tea, butter, sugar and soap and hand them over to the French Sisters of Charity who ran the hostel. The nuns were easily recognisable in their distinctive headdress. What was hard on us in the Training College was giving up our personal supply of coupons for materials, i.e. clothes. During our training we were expected to make blouses, skirts and other garments. As they were all rationed our own personal coupons were needed. Each person during the war had to have a personal ration book. The course consisted of Cookery, Needlework, Housewifery, Irish,

English, and Budgeting.

After three years I sat the final exam receiving my Diploma in Home Economics. This was followed by spending one further year in Dublin teaching in various Vocational Schools around the city.

During my time in Dublin I got to like the city. One had a great sense of freedom. One felt independent and I moved into digs in a house in Adelaide Road beside the Eye and Ear Hospital. Strangely enough I had been a patient in the Eye and Ear Hospital when I was about six having my tonsils removed.

I remember 1947 well as it was the year of the Big Snow. It was difficult to get around the city. On coming out of Mass one Sunday in Stephen's Green I slipped and fell in the snow, I wasn't the only one. It so happened that De Valera was also at Mass and his bodyguard came over and helped me up.

Coming to the end of the 1947 school year I applied for a job, which I saw advertised in one of the daily papers. The job was in Clonaslee, County Laois. I had never heard of Clonaslee. Mountmellick I had heard of because of the Boarding School there. It had a great reputation for Irish and Music. My knowledge was limited to Kilkenny and the South. I came for interview to Portlaoise. You were warned well in advance that any canvassing would automatically disqualify you. I remember little of the interview. On the board of interviewers was the head of the Vocational Committee in County Laois, the Principal of Portlaoise Vocational School and Oliver Flanagan TD.

I got the job. Later on the same day I met Pat Brickley, the Principal of the school. The teacher who had the teaching post before me was Beta Feeley. She stayed with Miss Lawlor who lived in Main Street up close to the Church of Ireland. I went to the October Devotions for the first time with Miss Lawlor. There was no electricity then so the streets were dark. The Church was lit up with candles around the sanctuary. As far as I remember the body of the Church was dark. Father Doyle led the devotions. After life in Dublin, Clonaslee was quiet. At the same time it was a busy village. Miss Lawlor, who was a dressmaker, was a very quiet refined lady. She seemed to have a fair number of customers. As it was wartime, in the sense that ration books were still in use, Miss Lawlor was constantly making renovations to existing garments. I am not sure if she was a native of Clonaslee but I do know when she became ill, she went to Abbeyleix Hospital where she died.

Christine Foley, Mairead's mother, on a visit to Holycross Abbey in 1939 with Mairead Corbet.

I arrived in Clonaslee during the first week of October. Classes had already commenced. After my first night at the devotions I called to Brickley's house to meet his wife Alice and baby son David. I was immediately struck by the resemblance of the baby to his father.

There were just three teachers on the staff: Pat Brickley,

Des Dillon and myself. My subjects were cookery, needlework, housewifery, Irish and English. My classroom was the kitchen where the pupils learned all about cooking. My classes were not too big as the enrolment was small. One of the main difficulties was that pupils could not travel and so pupils were all local. They were all expected to sit for the Group Certificate, which meant that they were all around sixteen years of age.

The following year I got married to Paddy Corbet from Ballykaneen. We got married in the Pro Catherdral, in the little chapel attached to it, known as St Kevins. In those days when you got married you retired from teaching, so I was only one year in the school. I did part time now and again. After I had my family reared, there were eleven children; I went back to teaching in 1969. My last son, Bob, had started Primary School in Castlecuffe.

There were now five teachers in the Vocational school. The number of pupils had increased. They could now sit for the Intermediate Certificate and there were also two extra rooms in the new prefab. Pupils now began to come from adjoining parishes, thanks to the new school transport policy. As well as teaching Home Economics I was now teaching English and Civics. One day in the Civics class we were discussing our duty to vote in elections. At the end of the class I asked the students *'Why should we vote?'* back came the answer, *'So that when we want anything they would have to get it for us'*. Everything appeared very simple.

With the arrival of rural electrification advances came in the farming world, housekeeping and the business world. Teaching practical classes in cookery benefited enormously. I now could teach and demonstrate to the students the advantages of having an electric cooker versus the range which I had used in the school when I first started back in 1947. In my time no boys ever came to cookery classes. They would have been looked upon as sissys, their realm being woodwork. First Year girls learned how to bake soda bread, scones and pastry. They then advanced to making sponge cakes, madeira fruit cakes, and Christmas cakes.

In the savoury dishes they learned how to make stews, omelettes, casseroles and roasts. So each student would leave the school well able to cook and housekeep. As far as I remember nobody went out to train professionally in this area. Of course, there was no Career Guidance in the schools back then.

I have seen many changes in the village over the years. Names have changed in the Main Street. Peavoys is still the same. Egans was doing big business when I arrived. Miss Guinan ran the Post Office while Mrs Webster ran the Church of Ireland School where Blooms Restaurant was later to open. Joe Conroy had a pub opposite the Post Office. Alongside was Feerys pub. Beside Mrs Webster's school was Dunne's Pub. This is now closed. With the arrival of supermarkets business has changed dramatically. People now can shop far afield as transport has become much easier. The passing of the Dublin bus was a big loss to the village.

Niall Corbet, great grandson of Mairead Corbet sitting with his Irish Under 18 International Cap 2012.

Paddy Kelly

Glimmer Man

PADDY KELLY, GORROUGH

I am a native of Dun Laoghaire and was born in 1931. It was then known as Dun Lock a Hair (phonetically Irish) where the famous boat train arrived. My earliest memories were of the bottle glass windows in our house. The back of the house looked out on what is now the Marina. People had boats there, a various selection of crafts, it was not as commercialised as it is now. The mail boat from Holyhead arrived in the morning and went out at night. There was always a full complement of passengers. It never sailed empty as jobs that time were scarce and England beckoned. I went to school in the local national school. It was a big school, three storeys high, with about four hundred boys.

I was in the Sea Scouts and all the activities that go with that organisation: sailing, rowing, and camping. I still know my Scouts Honour: trusting, loyal and helpful; brotherly, courteous and kind; obedient, smiling and thrifty; pure in body and mind. You did not have to be Protestant, Catholic or Jew to be a member! It was open to everyone. There were various troops all over the country. Our troop had about forty members. We were Boden Powell Sea Scouts as distinct from the Catholic Boy Scouts. Our salute was three fingers with the thumb and little finger folded over. It was really a great training for anyone. When we went away camping we had a Sunday morning service. It was neither Catholic, Protestant nor Jewish. We were involved in the Eucumenical movement way before Vatican II. If we were in a Catholic Church at the Gospel we always gave the salute with our right hand held high. We dressed in a full naval uniform complete with bell-bottom trousers. We wore a pillbox hat on our heads and around our neck we wore a neckerchief, fastened by a toggle, which looked like a serviette holder, fashioned in the shape of fleur-de-lis.

As Sea Scouts we got all the basic training in seamanship. You had to know all the sailing craft of the centuries, like the Tall Ships. You had to be able to send messages with two flags from one vessel to another - semaphore. For instance the angle of the flag was actually a letter of the alphabet so holding both hands straight out from the side of the body represented different letters. One also had to learn international code flags. They were run up in different sequences on to the mast. You would run up a sequence *sailing on the next tide.* The Blue Peter indicated *fever on board*.

Other activities included first aid, cooking, housekeeping, and maintenance of your craft. I would definitely recommend any scouting organisation for both boys and girls. It gives you comradeship, looking out for one another and while many places are inland as is Clonaslee there are land scouts as well.

I spent seven years with the Sea Scouts and I look back with great affection and fond memories to those years. Our headquarters were adjacent to the present Marina. Dun Laoghaire, in those days, was a small seaside town outside of Dublin. We all cycled into Dublin, Bray and the Wicklow mountains. You could park your bike anyplace and it would not be stolen. Going to the pictures, the Cinema in Dublin one could leave your bike anywhere from O'Connell Monument to Parnell at the other end.

A great way of getting into Dublin was by tram. The tram left from Nelson's Pillar passing Boland's Mills, Ringsend, Sandymount, Blackrock stopping at the promenade in Dun Laoghaire. The fare was sixpence in real old money but we could not afford it anyway. This was during the war years when people had no money, little food and gaslight. When the gas supply was low the gaslight went down to a glimmer. If you were caught by the Inspector using the glimmer - a mere trifle of gaslight - you would be prosecuted. Hence the title 'Glimmer Men' for the Inspector. The reason being that with the low pressure you could get 'blow back' causing an explosion as the low flame or spark could go back down the pipe to one of the junctions setting off an explosion.

My mother and father died within two months of each other in 1942. I then went to live with my father's sister in Blackrock continuing on in school until I was sixteen.

I have a distant memory of the bombing of the North Strand, by the Germans, during the war. A couple of days after the bombing my uncle and I went in to see the area. All I can remember is that at my age it looked horrific. It only took out an area as big as Clonaslee Village but to me it looked more. During that time as I was finishing my schooling I had a variety of odd jobs in the evenings. One of the jobs was making toy soldiers. Another job was bicycle courier, which involved delivering parcels from a depot to various parts of the city and surrounding county for two shillings and sixpence or half a crown. So the modern day courier is nothing new except they now have a big van. This gave me a great knowledge of the city and I could find my way anywhere even in the glimmer lighting. I also had a job with Film Distributions in Abbey St. This involved repairing the rolls of film, going to the Film Censor's Office, located in Abbey St., getting the *'Leader'*, permitting the film for general viewing, packing the films into steel boxes and then despatching them by bus or rail to all parts of the country. Posters for outside the cinema carrying the title of the film, *'Coming Soon'*, *'Now Playing'* were sent out with a synopsis of the film and the names of the stars. This job naturally gave me an interest in films.

Paddy Kelly in Kinnitty Castle.

By this time I was leaving off school and Bord na Mona, or the Turf Development Board as it was known then, had a recruitment campaign. This was around 1947, the year of the big snow. I got the train from Kingsbridge now known as Heuston Station down to Kildare. When I arrived in Kildare Town I asked a man where the bog was, never ever having laid eyes on a bog before. He told me there was no way of getting to it that night but there would be a lorry at 7 am the next day. He asked me if I had anywhere to stay so he brought me home to his house and put me up on the couch for the night. The next morning I went by open truck to Ballydermot bog in Rathangan ten miles from Kildare Town. The lorry was packed, standing room only. I was the only newcomer.

I was too young to start an apprenticeship being only sixteen years old, so the Camp Superintendent gave me a job in the kitchen peeling spuds by the ton. The Camp Superintendent was a Sligo man named Mr McGoldrick. There were hundreds of men in the camp, billeted mostly from the west of Ireland. I graduated from the spuds into the kitchen making soup, porridge, jelly and custard. There were meals going on all day. The day shift got breakfast and lunch packed. The night shift ate breakfast when they came in. The 4 pm shifts got dinner along with the night shift in the middle of the day. The morning shift returning at 4 pm got their dinner at 6 pm along with everyone else in the camp that got supper. This was a big organisation feeding at peak time during the turf cutting season a couple of hundred men. While in the wintertime there was only a skeleton staff to be fed.

Rathangan was a thriving village with the Post Office being the busiest place in town sending money to hundreds of homes by telegraph money orders. When I came of age I went as an apprentice to the workshop. In my spare time I was assistant medical officer, my training in the Sea Scouts coming in very useful. Most of the injuries were cuts and bruises along with sprained ankles, which I was able to handle.

In 1952 dancing was big in the Midlands, every little place having its own dance hall. I met my wife, at the local hop in Rathangan in Dockerys Hall, Miss Flynn of the local Post Office. After that we both went dancing two or three times a week. There were special occasions when the Show Bands came to one of the nearby towns within cycling distance. I can well remember dancing to Clipper Carlton, The Miami, Joe Dolan, who died recently, and The Drifters. Then there were the Dress Dances; long frocks, black suit and tie. Going to these dances involved cycling many miles there and back. Dances did not end until one or two o'clock in the morning and on the way home we had the hazard of the Gardai pulling you over for no lights on your bicycle.

Later that same year I was invited to Lil's home in Gorrough for Christmas. I arrived on Christmas Eve, after lunch. I cycled down from Rathangan through Bracknagh and Portarlington, a nice spin of thirty miles. I met Lil's mother and her two brothers Tom and John. The house was a hive of activity. Everybody was busy cooking, looking after the stock and chopping firewood for the two days. The ham was cooked but you couldn't eat it as Christmas Eve was a day of abstinence - I don't know how many can remember that! Being born in Dublin I was terrified of cattle. I thought every cow was a bull and was afraid to go near them. I was never as close to cows, horses, pigs, ducks, hens and dogs before.

On Christmas Day we set off for first Mass, in the dark on foot. There were throngs of people coming down the mountain. At that time a lot of families lived around the mountain all with nine or ten children. There has been a population shift to the village and adjacent areas since that time. Mass commenced at 8 am but everyone was there at 7.30 am. At that time everybody had their own family seat or pew in the Church. If you sat in the wrong one you were told to move. After Mass most of the relations met up, then back to Gorrough, breakfast and more work. I spent three days there and then back to Rathangan.

We began planning our wedding for September of 1953. My apprenticeship finished in February of that year. Then you were not kept on in the job, you had to leave. So I went to England with all the other thousands and I got a job on the oil refinery at Birkenhead, the other side of the River Mersey. I had a flat in Chester and travelled by train every day to Birkenhead. I got the job in the oil refinery easy enough. I had heard about the oil refinery going over on the boat. So I went and applied for a job and with my qualifications I succeeded. I continued working on in Birkenhead. Lil worked in other Post Offices around Ireland. We kept in touch by letter and phone until I came home for the wedding.

I arrived back in Ireland a few days before the wedding and travelled by bus down to Clonaslee. In those days we had a bus service from Dublin to Portumna taking in Clonaslee. It carried bicycles, luggage, day old chicks, evening papers and parcels as well as passengers. Kit Lynch was the driver and Jimmy Kelly was the conductor. It took about three hours from Dublin to Clonaslee calling to Kill, Johnstown, Portarlington, Mountmellick, and Rosenallis. The bus conductor, Jimmy Kelly, always called out Rose and Alice and the sky over it when the bus stopped there.

The wedding day turned out to be a wet and windy September morning. The wedding ceremony took place at 8 am with Father Ryan and Father Doyle officiating. I stayed in Mountmellick the night before while everybody in Gorrough was up at five o'clock doing the farm work and getting ready by candlelight. Up to then, wedding receptions were usually held in the bride's house but we broke with tradition and went to Kelly's Hotel in Portlaoise for the breakfast. At twelve o'clock they all saw us off on the train for Chester.

Paddy Kelly and his wife Lil

We stayed there until 1956 and then we came back to Clonaslee. Alfred, my son, was born the next year in 1957. Things had improved a little since the end of the war but conditions were still bad and wages were poor. The two big shops in the village, Williams and Egans had changed hands as well as the Post Office. If one was lucky enough to have a farm it provided most of the household needs. All one had to buy was tea and sugar and Stork margarine to make apple tarts. I travelled to follow the money, getting contract work wherever I could. When in England I availed of the opportunity to go to night classes. I studied Electrical Engineering and Automation. That was one of the reasons why I could always find work. The house in Gorrough was always very busy with neighbours, relatives and friends coming and going. It was one of the few houses with a radio. Neighbours would come to hear Michael O'Hehir broadcasting the match on Sundays. One Sunday Lil was tidying up after dinner, she had high-heeled shoes which went click, click, click on the flag floor. This man could not stand it any longer, he turned around and said *'Lizzie take off the heels and sit down'*.

Paddy and his son Alfred Kelly

We carried on like that until Alfred made his confirmation and he and I moved to Wexford where we had bought a house. Lil stayed at home to nurse her mother upon whom the years had taken their toll. We moved here permanently in 1976. I got involved with the Church in Father Kehoe's time looking after the heating in the Church and the schools. I'm still at it. Around that time Alfred and I began renovating the house. It was two hundred and fifty years old then and needless to say needed renovation. And we are still at it. The house is now in good shape.

So what do we gain and what do we lose? Seventy years ago ten shillings would keep you going for a week. Today money has no value. At that time we depended on God and the Church. We had sayings like: God willing, please God, help of God and thanks be to God when a task was well done. If you were going, after visiting a house, you got a blessing with a sprinkling of holy water, safe home and God be with you.

The Blake family reunited after 27 years in 1963. Mary Blake along with her family of twelve. Mary on the occasion said, *"The last time we were all together was in 1936 and then some of them were babies."*
Back row L-R: Gerard, Peter, Jack, Tom, Paddy, Jim, Mick and Martin.
Front row L-R: Tess, Mary, Mother, Winifred and Brigid.

On Mission

THE BLAKE FAMILY, GLENKEEN

Paddy's Story (Brother Mark)

I was born March 16th 1931 - number ten in a family of twelve, four girls and eight boys. We had a mountain farm, ten or twelve cows and calves which we kept till they were two to three years old and then drove them to the fair in Tullamore. I attended the Boys' National School in Clonaslee until I was fourteen. Then, instead of going to England to find a job like so many young Irish lads, I went to the Junior Novitiate in Castletown probably because my brother Tom had already gone there and a Brother came to Clonaslee looking for more boys to join. I spent two years in the Juniorate and then at sixteen went to the Novitiate. Then at the end of the Novitiate, I volunteered with five or six other novices for

Paddy Blake

the missions, mainly because I wasn't good at Irish and was afraid of finding the Inter Certificate and Leaving Certificate too difficult. After two years, I passed the Oxford School Certificate Examination and qualified to enter the teachers' training college in Strawberry Hill, Twickenham, London.

Two years later, after qualifying as a teacher, I was sent to the Far East. The journey by boat took about three weeks to Singapore. There my new Superior, Brother Fintan Blake, my cousin, a native of Clareen, Co Offaly, assigned me to teach at St Michael's, Ipoh, Malaya, now Malaysia, where my Director or Superior was Brother Denis Hyland from Cush, Clonaslee. His nephews Paddy and Sean went to school with me in Clonaslee. Whenever news came from home we were able to share it. Malaysia's independence from England was gained without having to fire a shot unlike Ireland. Looking back it's amazing how easily it happened.

The students, over ninety per cent Chinese, were very easy to teach as they studied hard in order to get good results and then good jobs. I spent eight happy years in Ipoh and was then transferred to Kuching, Sarawak, British Borneo. In 1983 I was sent to Hong Kong where I've been ever since. Everyone there was impressed with my love of sports especially rugby and athletics. It was once rumoured among students that I participated in the Olympic Games and no one doubted it! But I always said, *"That's not true. I can't even represent Kowloon!"* Kowloon was a team near the Chinese border. In 1993 I reached retiring age but continued to help in the school especially with the athletics teams.

Paddy Blake on the Great Wall of China

Retired now in Castletown, as I look back I have good memories of growing up. The fine people I met, not just in Clonaslee but all over the world. There was an old De La Salle brother from Vicarstown, Paul O'Connell who was in Hong Kong. He loved the Irish songs and when he sang *"A Nation Once Again"* it brought back nostalgic memories to us all.

Jack was the second youngest in the family, Peter being the youngest. Jack spent all his life in Glenkeen and ran the family farm. When I came home on holidays I stayed in what is known as *'Paddy's Shack'*. It was a hen house I turned into a small residence or retreat house.

Jack loved farming and always kept a few horses. Breeding and talking about horses was one of his main pastimes along with following Laois. Each year the house was painted to get ready for the family members who came home for a break.

The horses outside Paddy's Shack

We all missed my brother Jack greatly when he died. He always looked forward to our coming home and gave us a great welcome. He loved our company as the rest of the year he lived the life of a bachelor. When my sisters came home he really was in clover as it meant all the cooking was passed on to them and he loved home cooking.

During my holidays, I loved going to the GAA matches with Noel Foynes and Joe Young as I didn't drive and both men had great knowledge of the games and the players.

Over the years many changes have occurred in Clonaslee. The Church was always full for Sunday Masses. There were two masses at eight and eleven o'clock. There were no Saturday night masses then. I find it strange to see so few frequenting the church compared to my time. Vocations to religious life have fallen dramatically. Clonaslee had an awful lot of vocations in my youth, The Egans, O'Rourkes, Fitzpatricks and Hylands.

The village has even changed. There was only one car visible on the street, when I was young. There was a horse drawn hearse. My father was buried in Kilmanman. He died in 1942 during the Second World War. My mother was buried in the New Cemetery. In those years we had no electric light. I can remember when the lights were switched on. The wireless no longer needed a battery. We bought most of our groceries in Egans at the top of the village. Every two weeks my mother went in the pony and trap to Tullamore with country butter and eggs. It took us about an hour going by Gurteen Bridge.

On one occasion I remember walking the cattle to the fair in Tullamore. My eldest brother Mick and I left home about 3 am. We sold them in the Market Square, Mick often walking them home if he didn't get the price he wanted. There was never any trouble driving them home as they seemed to know their way. Going was the problem as they wanted to go into every field and open gap. Whenever Mick wanted to sell pigs he usually went down to the creamery in Clonaslee.

Peter went to live in Clareen where he farmed and married Cora English. He was fifty nine when he wed. Brigid married Chris Connors of Clareen. She had four children, three boys and one girl. Her husband Chris was a farmer. Brigid is at present in a Nursing home. Brigid's grandson, David Downey has built a new house on what was formerly Jack's land. David married Annette Maher and they had a baby boy recently. That is good as it means another family has come to live up the mountain in Glenkeen.

Tom's Story (Brother Lawrence)

I was born on December 1st 1929. In religion my name was Brother Lawrence. I served in many areas in South East Asia before I went to Hong Kong in 1958.

Tom Blake

One of the big memories during my school days was hearing the sound of a fire engine. This was a big event in the life of Clonaslee. It was the famous fire that burned down Brittas Castle, the home of the O'Dunnes. We were in school that day. Naturally there was great excitement in the village and the fire was reported all over Ireland. On our way home that day we saw the smoke as the Castle burned. At lunch time we all left without permission to go up and see the fire. I remember Guard Barry trying to get us back. We were very reluctant to go as the fire was more exciting than our lessons. Various stories abound as to the origin of the fire but the facts are unknown.

The caretaker's wife, Mrs Nash, often let us in around the Castle and orchard. We never had that much interest in it as we were too young. The apples, plums, pears and damsons all tasted good. Everything is good when you are hungry. The orchard extended over five acres. There was a lily pond in the orchard. There was a Mayor's Walk from the castle building to the lake named after Mayor O'Dunne. That walk is now overgrown. It came down from the castle, went along the present wall, crossed the road at the present bad turn into the shrubbery and down into the lake.

Years ago the hay was always left too late as there was very little manure to put on the land. This depended on the number of cattle you had, whereas now you could have forty cocks of hay due to the modern fertiliser, while then you would only have ten. Back then it was cut with two horses and a mowing machine. The hay was turned with forks by hand. If it rained it had to be turned several times. It was very difficult and time consuming. Nowadays with a tractor and hay bob it is much easier and quicker. You could say the same about the turf. Nowadays it is not cut by a slane but by a turf machine.

We used to go to the Fair in Tullamore, leaving at 1.45 am. We came down the mountain with the cattle through the village on to Cush and then into Tullamore. We aimed to be in Tullamore by 6 am. Sometimes we were lucky and sold some on the way in. North of Ireland buyers were mad for mountain cattle. They were four years of age, very thin, had their growth done in the mountains and so could be easily fattened. Glenkeen and Barradoo cattle were much sought after. Cattle in those times were never dosed, so when those cattle went to the North or down to Kildare, after they were dosed, they began to thrive. Our cattle, nowadays, would be classed as organic. We were before our time! In those days it was all mixed farming. Potatoes, oats, barley, turnips were all sown in most farms. People had to be self-sufficient. Everyone in their farmyards had hens, turkeys, geese, ducks and pigs. During the year the pig would be killed for household use. In our house all the girls and even some of the boys disappeared as we did not want to hear the pig squealing. The pig was cured, salted and then left on the floor with weights for two weeks, after which it was hung. It remained there until it was eaten. We had no fridge in those days and no electricity to begin with. As it was needed, a piece was cut off the flitch - one side of the pig - brought to the boil to take the salt out and then cooked for the dinner.

Of course we made our own butter and some milk went to the creamery in Clonaslee. Extra butter went to Tullamore. Our mother and Mrs Dunne, a next door neighbour, went by ass and cart to Tullamore to sell the butter along with eggs. On one occasion a jeep which had been built and put together by Jack Dunne and Jim Cleere came along the road making a horrendous noise. My mother jumped off the cart, put the shawl she had on over the ass's head so that the jeep would not frighten the ass and pass away. We always made our own bread in a baker, so, as you can see most people survived as they had to be self-sufficient.

The mountain is not the same now. Quite a lot of the old names have gone. They are not even in the parish, never mind being on the mountain. Names like: Cash, Wilks, King, Moys, Larges are no more. People were forced to leave the mountain as they were unable to survive. For instance two Buckley brothers left their house, never locked it, walked down the mountain one after the other and never came back. They went to Australia and were never heard of again.

My father used to go every evening over to Jimmy Conroy who lived near the Clodiagh River. There was a row every evening as only one of us was allowed to go with him and of course we all wanted to go. The reason being we got a very good meal of potatoes, butter, milk and onions known as colcannon. When we went over Jimmy would be saying the rosary. He would tie a piece of string on where he was so that he would know where to start when we had gone. Those days - which I regard as good days - are now all gone.

We had a relation Brother Fintan Blake who spent a good portion of his life in the Far East - Maylasia now. It was then known as Malaya. He always visited us when he came home on holidays.

Bother Leo Healy of Castletown often came around here on a bicycle to visit the schools. These two men had an influence on both Paddy and I.

Also Mrs Joe Conroy, who lived where O'Rourke's pub is now, had a brother who was also in the De La Salle congregation. He was Brother Gordan Maher. They originally lived up in Ballinalug, where Mrs Pat Dunne now lives.

When Brother Leo came out to visit he usually met us in Mrs Joe Conroy's house. She influenced many from around here including the two Fitzpatrick's from Tinnahinch, Brother Sylvester and Brother Fintan.

Paddy and Tom Blake

In 1943 and 1944 Paddy and I both went to the Novitiate in Castletown. I went from there to Mallow and then to Kilmacow while Paddy went to Kintbury in England. After taking Temporary Vows I went to Strawberry Hill for teacher training, while Paddy also went to Strawberry Hill. Our time there overlapped. We had to go there to qualify to teach in the English Colonies. It was difficult that time to get into Training College as many who had fought during the war were given preference. This was only fair and proper.

I became Principal of Chong Gene Hang College in 1987.

Prior to that I taught in La Salle College, Hong Kong. In 1995 I was transferred to Chan Sui Ki (La Salle College) where I taught until I was promoted to Principal. I am now the supervisor of both schools.

In my teaching years I taught English and Economics at O level. This would correspond in Ireland to Intermediate Certificate. Classes were through the medium of English. In all of the schools there were about nine hundred pupils. One of my regrets is that I never mastered Chinese. I could understand it but speaking and writing I found difficult.

I was fascinated by the Chinese culture and customs. I got the opportunity to travel widely in China and always felt that it was a slumbering giant. I am now retired in Hong Kong where I suffered a stroke in 2011.

The Blake Sisters

Teresa was born on November 4th 1928 the youngest of four sisters, Mary was born on April 15th 1917 and Winifred was born on January 19th 1919.

The Blake Sisters. Tess, Winifred and Mary

Mary entered the Convent of Mercy in Tullamore in 1934 and Winifred entered Bloomfield, Franciscan Convent in Mullingar. That Convent no longer exists as a Convent but is known as Bloomfield Hotel. Later Winifred went to Rome where she spent some years and then to America where, at various times, she lived in Philadelphia, New York, Chicago and is now living in Mount Alvernia Academia, Boston in retirement. She celebrated her ninetieth birthday on January 19th

Paddy and Winifred Blake with greyhound.

2009. She graduated from Boston College and taught in Mount Alvernia for many years and was happy to spend her retirement there, surrounded by many friends including Ciss Higgins, Brocca, who was a companion going to Bloomfield many years ago.

Teresa's Story

In 1934 my schooling began in St Brigid's National School, Clonaslee where I was taught, firstly by Mrs Jim Daly, a very kind teacher, and later by Mrs George Higgins and Mrs Bates. At that time I stayed with my aunt Mrs Daniel Hennessy at Bonastick so that I didn't have to walk from Glenkeen to Clonaslee, almost three miles each day. I went home to Glenkeen at the weekends.

Following Clonaslee Girls' School I went for a time to the Technical School in Clonaslee and then on to Clara where I was until 1945.

In 1946 I decided to become a Sister of Mercy. I had met some Mercy Sisters from Sunderland, a mining and ship building town in the North East of England, who gave a glowing report of life in England and convinced me that this was the place for me.

On March 5th 1946 I went by boat from Dunlaoghaire to Holyhead, travelling from Holyhead to Crewe by train; stayed overnight in Manchester and then went on to Sunderland the following day. On the way I saw the utter destruction of towns and buildings, the aftermath of the bombings of the Second World War. I began to get cold feet after leaving the green hills of Ireland behind. However, in Oak Lea Convent I was welcomed by a happy and lively group of 'Postulants', some from Ireland, some from Scotland and of course England with one from Italy. I was a Postulant for six months while deciding if this was the place for me and then received the white veil, which was the first step in my initiation into the life of a Sister of Mercy. Two years later I took the First Vows of Poverty, Chastity, Obedience and the Service of the Poor and Uneducated. After a period of study, and because we were a Teaching Order, I sat for Cambridge Certificate which qualified me for entrance into St Mary's Teacher Training College in Fenham and graduated from there as a qualified teacher in 1951. On returning to Sunderland I made my Final Profession as a Sister of Mercy. As time went on I studied for a Diploma in Administration Education Studies at Newcastle University.

My first job was in Saint Patrick's School, with children ranging from five years to fifteen years. There were three departments, Infant, Junior and Senior with three Head teachers. It was a very old school in the most deprived area of Sunderland and I taught there for eleven years.

The aftermath of the war was very evident. The bombed buildings had not yet been demolished and because it was the dock area of Sunderland it bore the brunt of the German bombings and of course the ship yards were their prime target.

Blake Family Wedding. L-R: Paddy, Tom, Winifred, John Maher, Carmel (Paddy's niece), Tess, Bid Connors and Jack Blake.

The children in the school were extremely poor, often coming to school without breakfast. The fathers and menfolk were absent, some killed during the war, others disabled and many still unaccounted for. There was no employment. On Saturdays it was our custom to visit the Open Market to buy rabbits which we distributed to the very needy for their Sunday lunch. The school was very overcrowded. In my first class I had forty five children.

Later, new housing estates were built and on every estate a Catholic School and Church sprung up relieving the overcrowding. I transferred to one of these schools, St Anne's, Pennywell. It was like heaven after the poor conditions of St Patrick's in the Hendon area. Many of the children in St Anne's had been my pupils in St Patrick's and so it was a happy time for all. Later I was in other schools in the Diocese of Hexham and Newcastle.

Conditions improved greatly as the years went by. Nowadays, few can imagine the utter dereliction of those days seeing the state-of-the-art housing and schools of today. Of course, ship building and coal mining, the chief employment of those days have gone and given way to other industries, one of which is the Nissan car factory where thousands are employed and of course the Stadium of Light has put Sunderland on the map.

In 1976, at the request of Bishop Davies of Ngong Diocese in Kenya, the Community released four sisters for direct Missionary work in Kenya. The immediate task was to found and run a Secondary School for Massai girls in Narok, a small "Wild West" town in West Kenya and help with both catechetical work for teachers and development work for women. The pioneering days were hard but greatly blessed and resulted in a flourishing school, St Marys, which is now in African hands.

It was the first school in Kenya for Massai girls, a semi nomadic tribe. The idea was to operate a rota of Sisters from Oak Lea Convent, Sunderland for about ten years or as long as necessary and then hand over to African teachers. I was one of four pioneers who first went to language school in Tanzania to learn Swahili, so we could communicate with the people.

During this time the Sisters left Narok in good hands and moved further into the bush to Lemek to teach in a newly founded Apostolic School. Now that task is completed and most of the Sisters are back except for three. One has remained to do medical administration, one joined an existing Community in Turkana and one is doing liaison work in Dafur, Sudan. It is her job to find placements for orphan children who live in the dreadful camp sites of Dafur and help with their education to build a new life.

I returned to Oak Lea Convent in the 1980's, and once again got involved in education in the Diocese of Hexham and Newcastle. On retirement I went to Gosforth, a suburb of Newcastle where I worked for six years and am now back enjoying my real retirement in Oak Lea, my Alma Mater Deo Gratis.

Bridie Flynn

Life is Like This, Sometimes Sun, Sometimes Rain

BRIDIE FLYNN, GLEBE

"We must educate that we may be free" –
Thomas Davis

It was the first journey of many I would set out on over the next nine years. My older brother and sister were taking care of me. I was on my way to enrol in Clonaslee Girls National School for the very first day.

We had travelled this journey every Sunday morning to 8 am mass with the pony and trap, but this day we were on foot. We met with many other boys and girls on our journey. We walked and talked and everything was going well until we reached the village side of Fawcett's hill. Suddenly we were caught in a shower of hailstones. One big boy called out *"All crowd round and save the new girl from the shower."* So, I was saved and we continued on to school.

I was enrolled in baby infants and spent four years in the junior room until I completed second class. My teacher for those years was Mrs. Daly. I liked being in school and I liked learning.

From third to seventh class inclusive I was taught by Mrs. K. Bates. The pupils in sixth class each year sat the Primary Certificate examination and duly got their certificates. Some pupils left primary school after sixth class while others continued on for another year or two.

When I was in seventh class I sat an examination at Easter time for the County Council scholarship. When the results of this examination were announced I was awarded a scholarship, which enabled me to study at St. Mary's Presentation College in Mountmellick for the next five years. During the nine years of primary education our teachers got to know us very well and we felt secure there and knew what was expected of us.

It was the same in our own home. I was the fourth child in a family of nine. My parents had to work diligently to rear a big family. There was work to be done in the house, in the farmyard and the various seasonal activities in the fields. As each of us children grew up we were given tasks to do. Some of us were given indoor tasks while others were given outdoor tasks. We helped with planting and picking potatoes, thinning turnips, preparing animal feed and all the various chores - bringing in animals or putting them out to graze. During the summer days there was plenty of hard work to be done in the hayfields but it could be great fun as well. That was described as *"clean work."* Soon after the haycocks were made they had to be made safe in case they were blown over in a storm. This activity was called *"heading the cocks."* My father had a hay twister, which he made himself, and this was used for making hay ropes to secure each haycock.

Whenever work was in progress in the fields a member of the family brought out the four o'clock tea - freshly baked scones with home made butter and plenty of tea. It always tasted so much better than the food served in the house. Of course it was also a rest from the hard work in progress. In the summer evenings we played outdoor games - hide and seek, skittles, hop the ball and football. In the winter evenings we played board games and cards or listened to the radio. The radio was also very popular on Sunday summer afternoons listening to whichever match was broadcast.

Perhaps the highlight of the farming year was the threshing day. The big tractor and threshing machine arrived the evening beforehand. It was a real hive of activity in the house and in the haggard. Extra men had to be fed, perhaps as many as fifteen. Extra food had to be prepared and cooked. There was plenty of lemonade and orange juice to drink and something stronger, for those who had a liking for it, to slake the thirst. The good and kind neighbours supplied all the extra hands to deal with the different tasks pertaining to the threshing. Some were pitching the sheaves, cutting the twines, pitching the straw, making the rick and very importantly some very diligent men were looking after the golden grain filling the sacks. All the time the hum of the thresher and the smell of T.V.O. filled the air.

In the 1940's and the 1950's we had a Pipe Band in Clonaslee parish. It was lovely to watch this band and to listen to the music as they paraded up and down the Main Street on St. Patrick's Day. Also, another open-air entertainment known as *"An Aeríocht"* was held in either Conroy's field or Brady's field. Fun and games, competitions, music and dancing were on the menu for the afternoon and it was thoroughly enjoyed by young and old. One particularly big achievement of the people of the parish in the 1950's was the building of the *"Curate's House"* through voluntary labour. In the summer of the same year there was a day of celebration when Bishop Keogh came to the parish for the blessing of the new house and handing over of the key to the Reverend Father Thomas Doyle.

In September 1951 I commenced my studies at St. Mary's College. As well as bearing the title "St. Mary's College" I soon learned that it was the "College of Our Lady of Victories." Living in the college and going to class in the same building was an enormous change. Three hundred boarders in uniform was a great spectacle as they walked from the college to the parish church for 7.30 am mass from Monday to Friday and again as they processed to the college chapel for rosary and prayers in the evening time. The school was well known as a school where high standards were maintained and excellent results were achieved. Photographs of past students who had achieved great results hung on the walls and this was a reminder to us to pick up the baton and carry on.

I met some lovely friendly girls there who had come from the three provinces of Leinster, Munster and Connaught. We stood by each other and were loyal in all the ups and downs of our five years. I recall very well how skilful the girls from Mooncoin and Kilmacow were on the camogie field. Also, there was a student from the Aran Islands whom I liked to hear speaking our native tongue with the lovely "blas".

During the 1950's students normally spent five years in secondary education. The term "Transition Year" had not yet come into our vocabulary. After two to three years we sat the Intermediate Certificate examination and at the end of the fifth year we sat the Leaving Certificate examination. There were many opportunities available to students in St. Mary's College. They had opportunities to learn languages; Irish, English, Latin and French. They had opportunities to learn science subjects; General Science, Chemistry and Physiology. Also available to us were; History, Geography, Mathematics, Commerce, Needlework, Cookery and Religious Education. The school had two three-part choirs as well as a junior and a senior orchestra. Many of the students practised piano, violin, viola, cello or double bass. The girls took examinations on these instruments annually and many achieved excellent results.

Pupils from Reary School celebrating at the school in 1974, with their numerous medals, plaques and the coveted trophy which they won at the Festival on the Mountain.

As a student, my ambition was to become a Primary teacher. So, after completing my Leaving Certificate I continued my studies in Carysfort Training College, Blackrock, County Dublin to train as a Primary teacher. At that time only girls attended Carysfort. All students dressed in the college uniform and lived in the college, which was managed by the Sisters of Mercy.

Our days were very busy in Carysfort. We started with the ringing of a very loud bell at 6.15 am and remained busy until 10 pm each night. We had some free time on Saturday afternoons and sometimes on Sunday afternoons when we could explore the city or get involved in other recreations.

Music was a key subject in Carysfort, just as it had been in St. Mary's College. Choir was an important part of college life. Pupils who wished to practise a musical instrument got the opportunity to do so. The college had a beautiful concert hall where, among other performances, students watched Our Lady's Choral Society perform *"The Messiah"*. Students also used the Concert Hall nightly at recreation time for modern and Irish dancing.

I met students from many counties of Ireland in Carysfort. Many of them came from Gaeltacht areas and had attended preparatory colleges. At this time I became aware of the Donegal dialect, the Dingle dialect and the Connemara dialect.

The college was a fine building in the 1950's. It was located on a good farm and we could see the contented animals grazing there as we went from lecture to lecture and attended to our studies. Sadly, it ceased to exist as a Teacher Training College, and the last student teachers to complete their studies there were the class of 1988. It now houses the Smurfit Business School and the rolling fields have been covered with modern buildings.

My first teaching appointment was in Kinnitty National School. I spent most of my teaching career in schools of a similar size with the longest appointment being in Reary National School in Rosenallis. For the greater part, school days were happy and challenging. But as the proverb says; *"life is like this, sometimes sun, sometimes rain"*.

L-R: Nancy Costello, Bridie Flynn and Jim Costello in Costello's award winning garden.

In 1989 the parish priest of Clonaslee, Father Joe Shortall, invited the parishioners to form a choir in preparation for the ordination mass of John Brickley. A group of people duly came together for that purpose and I was one of them. Sister Celine Conway prepared the choir for the ordination and conducted the choir for the ordination mass and again for Father John's first mass. John Brickley's ordination to the priesthood by Dr. Laurence Ryan, Bishop of Kildare and Leighlin, took place in Clonaslee on the June 18th 1989. It was a wonderful and memorable occasion for the whole parish.

The church choir, which was formed on that occasion, has continued now for twenty years. We sing at mass on Saturday evenings and at many funerals in the parish. I have been involved with the choir since its formation.

While I attended Clonaslee Girls National School I made my first Confession and received my First Holy Communion in St

Manman's Church. When I was in Fifth Class I was confirmed by Bishop Keogh in St Manman's Church. Tom Flynn from Reary Valley and I, Bridie Dunne from Clonabeg were married in St Manman's Church in 1964. We bought a site on the front field of the Rectory land and employed Denis Foynes of Ballinakill to build a bungalow. We have one daughter named Sinéad.

Dunne and Flynn families at the wedding of Bridie and Tom Flynn in 1964.

Sinéad celebrated her marriage to Niall Doran in 1997 in St Manman's Church with Father Joe Shortall officiating and Father Brendan Supple concelebrating. Sinéad and Niall now live in South County Dublin with their two children. My husband Tom was employed by Clonaslee Co-op Society from 1963 and continued to work there up to his retirement. Tom's hobbies and pastimes were all sports related especially hurling and gardening. He won Junior, Intermediate, and Senior medals with Clonaslee. Each year he won prizes at the Clonaslee Show with produce from his garden.

There are many opportunities available to parishioners who wish to participate in church life in Clonaslee. I have been privileged, particularly since my retirement from teaching, to be able and willing and to have the time to make a contribution to parish life. Buíochas Mór Le Dia.

Fred Mathews

The Co-Op

FRED MATHEWS, BELLAIR

I was born in Killoughey, Co Offaly in 1932. I went to school in Clonaslee in the Dunne Memorial School which was located on the Main Street. It was run by Mrs Jessica Webster. She was born in 1903 in the same house which was also the school. Her father was Richard Patterson who was born in Ballyshannon, Co Donegal. He was brought down by a group of Scotch Presbyterian farmers to teach their children at the Blacklion. He was only eighteen at the time. The Dunne Family, all of their retainees were Church of Ireland, wanted to start a school for them so they got the premises ready which today is Bloom's Restaurant. They offered Richard Patterson £50 to come and teach in Clonaslee. It was a lot of money at the time. He taught in the school from 1892 to 1932, then his daughter Jessica came back from teaching in Canada to take over. She continued teaching in the school until it was closed in 1971. Jessica's sister and her brothers lived well into their nineties.

The war years and petrol rationing meant that I had to leave and go to Mount Bolus School. At the time there was transport from Killoughey Cross to Clonaslee run by Seamus Bourke, an uncle of the present Pat Bourke. Seamus lived at that time a few doors up from the school. In 1945 I went to boarding school in Wilsons Hospital, Multy-farnham. I sat my Intermediate Certificate in the Franciscan Friary. Then I went to Mountjoy School, Dublin for one year. The school moved that year to Mount Temple Compre-hensive School, Howth Road, where I did my Leaving Certificate. It is now known as the

Fred Mathews on O'Connell Street, Dublin 1952.

school where Bono started his band. During my time in Mount Temple I played rugby against Tony O'Reilly amongst others.

When I left school, my father, being disillusioned with the economic war and farming, did not encourage me to go back to the land. So I went to work in Salts Woollen Mills in Tullamore. I hated every minute of it so I returned to farming in Killoughey.

I met my wife, Ena Furlong, in the early fifties. We got married in 1955 and moved to Clonaslee. Immediately I became involved with the Clonaslee Show and Macra na Feirme. I am still very much involved with the Show and am one of the longest standing members.

To the detriment of Macra the committee put all their endeavours into forming the Co-operative Piggery. This became one of the most travelled committees in the country. We travelled all over Ireland, north and south, looking at piggeries. Those still living from that great committee are Jim Costelloe, Henry Dunne, Chris Horan and Michael Dunne. Those who have passed on and gave great service were P.D. Brickley, who was Chairman all along, Paddy Corbet, Bill Flynn, Father Fleming, Dr Leahy, Joe Malone and Eric Greene. In 1961 Richard Davis' farm in Corbally came on the market. I, myself, happened to be executor to his will. As Secretary to the Co-op group we bought it for £10,000.

We were guided by the I.A.O.S. - Irish Agricultural Organisation Society in Merrion Square who were founded by James Plunkett. Their representative, James Joyce, who was from Tullow, Co. Carlow, was one of our mentors in looking for an architect. The I.A.O.S. recommended an architect called Colm Dickson who was a successful private architect in Dublin but had no knowledge of agriculture, especially pigs. He supplied plans for the first two original pig houses, which the committee put out to tender. The contract was won by Martin Turley, Builder, Portarlington.

Fred Mathews on the tractor with his brother Raymond Mathews on the reels.
On the sacks are Joe Dunne and Tom Smith in 1959.

The first stage for production was ready by 1963. From 1961, when the farm was purchased, we cleaned up the place, sowed barley and did some drainage. Ned Smith of Chapel Street was the first employee. We sold the barley to Donaghmore Co-op as they were our major shareholders. We had to collect money in the beginning via shareholding from all local farmers and business people. The more shareholding we got, the greater the bank input into the project. The Bank Manager of the National Bank in Mountmellick was of great assistance. As well as collecting share capital we were also trying to encourage all our members to build sow units on their own farms. This would ensure a constant supply of weaned pigs without having to go to the open market. The prevalence of disease in the market influenced us in this decision.

I became manager in 1963. The starting salary was £720 a year rising to £999. We had two members from Donaghmore Co-op and two members from Roscrea Bacon Factory at every meeting, they assisted the local committee. They were invaluable as we were a fledgling Co-op.

The next employees were Tom Flynn of Glebe and Terry McRedmond. The first pigs came in - four - on October 8th 1963. At that time we did not have our own milling plant. We got all our meal from Donaghmore Co-op and some from Rath Co-op between Tullow and Shillelagh. I did two weeks training in that Co-op before I became Manager. We converted the existing hay shed into our own milking plant which was built by Henry Dunne. All of the machinery was supplied by Semac of Cork. Jack Conway of Castlecuffe was the next employee and he worked the milling plant. The meal was sold on the premises to our producers.

During all these formative years we learned that the original buildings were not a good design and were much too expensive. Cost per head was increasing and we did not have a viable number of pigs. Our financial structure with the Agricultural Credit Corporation, A.C.C., had not been fully thought out so difficulties in day to day running of the Co-Op began to emerge.

I resigned in 1968 and was replaced by Tom Hennessy, who revolutionised the place. He was a good business man and an expert in beef production, as well as pig production. He now lives in County Cavan.

Co-ops played a big part in the rural development of this country. They began in the neediest areas such as West Cork, Monaghan, Leitrim and Mayo. As new global business enterprises began to emerge, the large ones began to take over all the smaller co-ops and so today we have Glanbia and Kerry Co-op.

I had a life changing experience in 1966 which led to my hospitalisation in St Patrick's Hospital, Dublin under the care of Dr Moore. My stay there was very beneficial and fruitful and incidentally saved me a huge amount of money in the future as I was refused V.H.I. membership due to my stay in St Patrick's.

After leaving the Co-op, due to my aversion to abattoirs and cattle marts, my farming directed me towards sugar beet and cereals. I grew twenty acres of sugar beet each year and during the campaign drew four wagons of beet to Tullamore Railway Station which were sent to Tuam Sugar Station. I also drew sugar beet to Mountmellick Railway Station. At this stage East Cork Foods contracted farmers in this area to grow brussels sprouts. This continued for a few years and gave intense employment. When East Cork Foods closed up I continued and increased my sprout growing and got a contract with Five Star and Lipton Group in Dublin. I grew up to eight acres of sprouts which we processed here in the barn and had eight to ten people employed when times were bad. I sold these sprouts in the Dublin market. Eventually a merchant in the Dublin Corporation Market at Smithfield went bankrupt and brought me with him. I then switched my farming from sugar beet to potatoes and unfortunately in 1977, when I had forty acres of potatoes, the market collapsed. When that happened - bankrupt again. To salvage something from this disaster I rented a premises in Mountmellick, which is now Hacketts Bookie Office and started a fish, fruit and vegetable shop. I bought all my fish from Giles Brothers, who were uncles of Johnny Giles, Irish International and now soccer pundit. That shop was a success but I had to leave it in 1987 and I moved down nearer to the Roman Catholic Church. Due to the untimely death of Tom Smith and my son leaving the business, I found myself back at square one again.

Gradually I withdrew from farming and became involved in interior decorating, painting - which I liked, and other pursuits. When I closed the shop I started as a contract meter reader with E.S.B. Starting with a small area I eventually built a large area, twice the usual area, starting with Clonaslee and extending as far as the Cush Inn in Kildangan, Co Kildare, including the towns of

Mountmellick, Portarlington, Monasterevan and as far as Stradbally. This was a massive area to cover. During this period I made many new friends and got a wonderful insight into the lives of thousands of people. When I finished I had approximately ten thousand households on my books. When I started meter reading, books were a matter of addition and subtraction involving thousands of leaves screwed together. This eventually evolved to electronic handsets which were loaded and unloaded on modems which is the system used today. This saved travelling to Portarlington with numbers of bulky books and it meant that I had the office at home in my own room and never had to meet my boss. Today there are at least four people covering the same area I did. I had to stop in 2006 after twenty three years due to family illness.

Fred Mathews daughter Irene's wedding, was the last wedding held in what is now the Heritage Centre, which will be 200 years old in 2014.
L-R: Ian Mathews, Clive Crampton, Ena Mathews, Charles Crampton, Irene Mathews Crampton, Fred Mathews, Cheryl Crampton, Freda Mathews.

When I first came to Clonaslee there were quite a few Church of Ireland families. In fact Clonaslee parish had its own Rectory, now owned by Dick Underwood. I, in fact, sold it to Dick.

The Church was endowed by the Dunnes of Brittas at £150 a year. Back in that time this was a good salary for a clergyman. When I came here the Rector was Reverend Frank Skuse who married Ena and I. Parishioners at that time were: Faulkners of Castlecuffe, three families of Furlongs, Fawcetts, Lees, Peavoys, Websters, Hipwells, Kershaws, Davis' and Mathews.

Due to the drop in numbers parishes were amalgamated. Clonaslee joined up with Rosenallis, Coolbanagher and Mountmellick. Eventually numbers had dropped down to about five families which just could not support the upkeep of the church.

The Representative Church Body decided to close Clonaslee Church completely. In 1990 during a vacancy in the parish, Bishop Robert Empey had a de-consecration service and that was the end of our church as a place of worship.

The Representative Church Body, when they went to sell the church, discovered a clause in the deeds of the Church that if it ever ceased to be a place of worship it was to revert to the Dunne's of Brittas Estate which at this time was also defunct. It took four to five years before this could all be resolved and eventually it was auctioned in 1994. The Community Council bought it at a public auction for £9,000. The outcome was welcomed by those of us who were left as we now knew the building would be restored and kept as a local landmark.

The very last chapter of the Dunne's of Brittas happened when, the last surviving member, Miss K.P. Dunne's ashes arrived by post to Mrs Webster. She died in a nursing home in Sulfolk and was cremated at Ipswich. Mrs Webster and I buried her urn in the cemetery in Brittas grounds on April 20th 1960.

When I was seven years old I started to collect stamps. As

a schoolboy I found that stamp collecting was a tremendous advantage in history and geography. A stamp collector knows where any place is on the globe. Many countries issue colourful stamps of their native flora and fauna. In my youth I actually dealt in stamps and had about a hundred Approval Books out to schoolboys all over the country through advertisements in the comics of the day such as *The Wizard* and *The Hotspur*.

Fred and Ena Mathews at a cider wheel in Jersey.

Since coming to Clonaslee in 1955 I have always been deeply involved with the Clonaslee Show. At that time the I.C.A. and Macra na Feirme ran the show in the old Vocational School. There was no livestock that time. When the show expanded, Macra and I.C.A. combined to form the Show Committee. The building of the new Community Centre allowed the Show to expand in many new directions.

It was always my hope to include art in the Clonaslee Show which proved very successful and has added a whole new dimension to its growth. I was a late starter in artwork and am self-taught. My main medium is watercolours. Nearly all my family paint as well. My chief loves are seascapes, landscapes and some wild life. I do not paint to sell or make money. Believe it or not I have paintings in fifteen countries at least. I started a good few art groups through the I.C.A. and Women's groups. I taught art also for a while but I had to stop as very few art groups want to use watercolours as a medium.

Painting is very therapeutic and peaceful. Personally I come alive in the early hours of the morning. All my best paintings have been produced between 1 am and 3 am.

I feel proud that I had a hand in introducing painting to the local area and the show. At each show we get sixty to seventy entries covering abstract, land or seascape, wildlife and portraits.

Ena and I were very fortunate to have property surrounding the village. We felt it a privilege to have helped many people to start business and get their own homes. If I leave Clonaslee a better place for having paused here for sixty years in my life's journey, then it has been a successful life.

Bridie O'Brien

The Little Phantom

BRIDIE O'BRIEN, BALLINAHOWN

I was born in Scaroon, a townsland up the mountain. Back in 1934 there were plenty of houses in the locality. There are only eight families there now. In my time there were at least twenty two families with plenty of contact between us. My father died when I was six. As there were seven of us, my mother had a difficult time rearing us. I can barely remember my father, Martin Delaney. My brothers, Tom and Mick were ten and twelve years old so my mother's two brothers Pat and Mat, along with the neighbours, helped us out as much as they could. We all walked down to school each day along with the other local children. So we got to know each other well.

I met my husband Tom at a dance in Portarlington, which was a benefit dance in aid of the Lourdes Fund. The dance was organised by Ina Wrafter. Their pub on the Main Street has recently been sold to a man from Rosenallis.

I came to live in Ballinahown in 1971. At the beginning I found it lonely until I got to know the neighbours. Our house is in County Laois beside what is known as the County Bridge which divides us on the map from County Offaly. On the main road to Cadamstown there is a sign for *The Giant's Grave* which brings visitors past our house. We get many people calling, inquiring for its where abouts. It is approximately one mile through Siskeen Forest from our front door. Local folklore has it that a very big man is buried there: *Giant Daly.*

Tom, my husband, was a great man with machinery. Farmers from many counties came to him to fix combines, boilers, and tractors. He would be called out at night time to fix all makes of cars. Many could have broken down on the road. He had marvellous hands and a great brain. Carpentry was also one of his many trades. All the furniture in the house, presses, tables, glass cases were made by him. He also built our own house from top to bottom. He had a great interest in how machinery functioned. Tom loved exploring and fixing radios, watches and clocks. His fame spread far and wide and an article about him featured in one of the local papers at the time.

John Moran had been working in the Forestry for a number of years and in 1962 he bought what was known as Dunne's Garage on the main street beside the Clodiagh River. Joe and Jimmy Dunne, as well as running the garage, had lorries drawing timber. They also drew corn at harvest time. It was Jimmy's son,

Francis, who sold the garage. John had saved up money from his time in the Forestry. There was a little field at the back of the garage, a little over two acres. The auctioneer, Joseph Morgan of Mountmellick advised John not to let the field go to anyone else as he would need a right of way through the yard. He paid £500 for the field and £1,600 for the house and garage.

At Moran's Garage. L-R: John Moran, Tom O'Brien and Damien Moran.

Two years later, 1964, my husband Tom went to work in the garage and remained there for thirty four years until in 1998 he became ill. Through their work they became very close. Tom's younger brother Jack left Kelly's in Portlaoise to come to work as well and he remained until his death in 1995.

John Moran always said that Tom O'Brien was a genius and that he knew a lot about cars. He made a toy threshing mill which was worked by a little engine using methylated spirits. The paper did an article on it with the title *'Tommy is proud of the Little Phantom'*. It tells about the made-to-scale working model of a threshing mill made by Tom. It really threshes and is complete in every detail. Many hundreds have seen it in action, powered by a small motor or miniature steam engine. Tom lost count of the number of hours he spent *"on and off"* making the model, but he got great satisfaction out of seeing it run. It kicked up a nice racket as the tiny components chugged away in exact imitation of the rumbling mill from which it was copied. It may well be called *"The Little Phantom"* as it is modelled on a threshing mill which became

Tom O'Brien with the model steam engine and threshing machine.

famous because of a story about it which originated at Cadamstown. The radio had it at the time that without human aid the threshing mill moved from its roadside position into a field ready for threshing operations. A local bard composed a few verses about the episode and it became well known to the local people.

The most common cars in Clonaslee then were Ford Escort, Austin A40, Morris Minor and the Volkswagon Beetle. There was a car at the time that was known as N.S.U. My husband Tom christened it: *No Shagging Use!*

The shop on the Main Street at the side of the garage as well as selling car parts and petrol was also a great social centre. Many customers, Tom Higgins among others, were regular visitors. The shop was also a great card playing spot, 25's being regularly played. On one occasion a man came in to buy a fan belt around 9 am. He left at 4 pm. When asked *"how did he get on,"* he replied, *"That was a very dear fan belt."*

I had four sisters. Teresa, Josie, Kathleen and Mary. Teresa became a nun. She joined the Franciscan Order and has spent most of her life in Little Hampton, Sussex. Josie lives in Newtownforbes, Longford and has three children. Kathleen lives in Ballinasloe, she worked all her life in Brown Thomas, Grafton Street. She enjoyed her work there. Mary is married in Ballinasloe and has four children.

As young children, the five of us girls helped our mother on the farm. Each morning before we went to school we milked the cows. As there were no electric kettles or ranges then we lit the fire on the open hearth each morning. Our mother taught us how to bake bread in the baker. The baker was a round pot with a handle which hung over the fire from a crane. We baked every day for the family. The potatoes, vegetables and all the food was cooked on the open fire. There was a little hob on both sides of the fire. There was often many a row as to who could sit on the hob, the reason being that it was nice and warm sitting there.

Neighbours in Scaroon Brigid Hogan and Bridie O'Brien.

At night time, Mick Kearney and Mick McCann, our uncles, would come. They would sit on the hob and we would be put to bed. We were not permitted to listen to what they were talking about. Our grandmother lived with us. She died two years after our father in 1948. My father was only fifty three when he died.

Our mother taught us how to sew. Washing clothes was done with the washboard and the bath. She also showed us how to make an apple cake. The pastry, which was thicker than now, was put into the baker first. Then the apples were put on top of the pastry which was then covered with another layer of pastry. The lid covered the baker and red coals from the fire were put on the lid. The crane then held the pot over the fire for about half an hour until the apple cake was cooked. It was a big apple cake - at least twice the size of the ones now. It was moved onto a big dish. As there was also juice on the bottom we all got spoons to sample the juice after we had eaten the apple cake.

Our mother taught us everything about cooking. Scones were made by using a cup or glass to cut them from the dough, unlike the cutters used today.

I loved eating the bread and scones when they were hot. We made our own butter. We churned every week, usually on a Monday and the butter had a lovely yellow colour and a salty taste. One of our jobs was to go around picking up the eggs every day. We reared a few turkeys for Christmas and we always had a goose as well.

My four sons, Thomas, Martin, Kevin and Brendan seem to have inherited all of my husband's talents along with some of their own. Some of the lads went to school in Cadamstown as well as Castlecuffe and Clonaslee. Cadamstown School closed in 1983/84.

Kevin has a great interest in clocks, and engines. At an early age he loved nothing better than to open the back of a clock, put the parts on the table and try to reassemble it, much like other children would like to assemble a jigsaw. He loved reading magazines about machinery, especially tractors. This is his occupation now. He works in Emo at the John Deere Garage. His work includes going around the country repairing John Deere tractors and machinery. He was always interested in cars and loved looking at vintage cars of all makes. Going to vintage rallies is one of his great joys.

All the O'Brien family at the Stradbally Steam Rally. L-R Back row: Tom with Brendan in his arms and Bridie. Middle row: Thomas. Front row: Martin and Kevin with monkeys on their shoulders.

Martin has a great interest in astronomy. He got this from his father who loved pointing out the different stars. From an early age all of the boys, on starry nights, would look for the

Plough, the Great Bear and the Small Bear. He bought various books which increased his interest all the more. I know that he has a telescope and on a fine night he loves nothing better than focusing it on the sky.

Brendan started off as a mechanic on tractors in Shaws of Rosenallis. From that he went on to work on generators. He went to work for McCormack - McNaughton at the generator hire business. He was often called out at night time to a break down. At present he is installing generators on the Shell to Sea Pipeline in County Mayo.

Thomas is also into machinery. His main occupation is driving. He works for Grennans of Rath delivering feedstuff all over Ireland. It can involve many long hauls on the road. Thankfully none of the boys have had accidents. Thomas is also involved in vintage trucks and takes part in vintage rallies. Thomas participates in the vintage rally held in Clonaslee every year.

When the present altar in St Manman's Church was being erected Tom and his brother Jack were called upon to give a helping hand putting it into place.

Joe Young

Fifteen Popes

JOE YOUNG, CHAPEL STREET

The earliest memory I have of Clonaslee is 1937, St Stephen's Day, the reason being that my aunt brought a message to Clonaslee from a woman in Portlaoise who lived in the house where Pauline and Tom Horan now live in the Square. It was just after my fifth birthday, 6th December. I remember that incident because my Aunt was dressed in black and was terrified of the Wren Boys who at that time came in droves to Clonaslee.

I was trying to get under her black coat to get away from the Wren Boys because I was also frightened. There was a man on the bridge called Delaney, it was a hump backed bridge then and he said, *"He will never go with the Wren anyway".*

As years went by I ended up going out with the Wren Boys and accompanying them all over the place. On St Stephen's Day we visited the mountain and then the village at night time. We usually put black on our faces covered by masks to hide our identity. We carried holly bushes, which we cut the week before and decorated with colour paper, which was taken off the Christmas cake. Our opening song at each hall door was:

'The Wren, the Wren, the king of all birds.
St Stephen's Day she was caught in the furze.
Up with the kettle and down with the pan.
Give us your answer and let us be gone.'

Wren boys from Kinnitty, Rosenallis, Mount Bolus and Killeigh descended on Clonaslee all during that day. It was often known that the big boys robbed the small boys when they met them. So we used to put the pennies in our shoes, which we had gathered with the Wren.

I started school around 1938. I didn't like school even though Mrs Dunne was a nice teacher. She was the mother of broadcaster and journalist Mick Dunne who wrote for the Irish Press. I didn't like leaving her and going out to the other room. Mrs Dunne was a native of Bagenalstown. There were about ninety boys in the school, ten being in my class. A lot of my classmates are now dead. At least half of those boys went to work in England.

During the war years there was no way of travelling except by bike. So all the Mass servers during the week were from the village. Your turn would come every five weeks, two designated for the 8 am morning Mass. Father Doyle was the Curate so he did most of the work as Father Murray had become very feeble. He was here as Parish Priest from 1913 to 1947, a fair stretch and was a native of Castledermot. In his latter years he was too feeble to go up on the High Altar so he said Mass at the Blessed Virgin Altar and it usually took him around an hour. This suited us as Altar Boys as we missed the first class in school, not arriving in class until 10 am so missing Irish and spelling.

I finished school at Christmas 1946. That summer was as bad as this one. The Army was mobilised to go out and help the farmers to save the harvest. Everybody was drafted in, shopkeepers, teachers, and people from Dublin as it was a crisis situation. From the beginning of the War there was compulsory tillage. Each farmer had to sow a percentage of his farm with wheat as nothing could be imported.

Really I should have started in the Vocational School in September of that year. I can remember Jim Young coming to the teacher to bring me down to the Technical School as they were anxious for more pupils. But the teacher would not release me until I reached my fourteenth birthday. I came to an abrupt end in the Primary School as it closed mid-December due to an outbreak of measles.

Oranges came again to Clonaslee in that year. I remember vividly making a glutton of myself with what money I had at D.E. Williams shop. They were stored in crates, two sections with coloured paper to separate them. They came from Spain and South America.

In January 1947, I went in the snow for the first time to the Technical School. I remember a teacher telling me that it was not a Technical School but a Vocational School, but there was a Technical School in Portlaoise. At the beginning it was a big change and I found it very hard to settle in. There was Woodwork, Science, Rural Gardening and Bookkeeping which was strange and there was a mountain of homework. To the best of my knowledge there were about fifteen pupils and some of them dropped out.

Looking back I can see why Jim Young wanted me to enrol as there must have been a danger of the school closing. However there was a very good attendance at night classes, especially the woodwork, cookery and needle classes. The two male teachers were Mr. Brickley and Mr. Dillon. Miss Foley came in September from Kilkenny. She was to settle down in Clonaslee as Mrs Paddy Corbet and now lives in Ballykaneen. Mr Brickley taught Irish, Science, Rural Science, Commerce or Bookkeeping while Mr. Dillon taught Woodwork, Mechanical Drawing and Maths. Miss Foley taught Cookery and Needlework to the girls as well as English. There was one other teacher who left the following summer. Her name was Miss Feeney.

The old creamery where River View houses now stand. Alongside, painted in white, is Malachy Cusack's Grocery and Hardware Shop.

I spent three and a half years in the school. I did get the opportunity to take up an apprenticeship in the Air Corps and the Sugar Company and I always regretted not taking it. I was a bit shy and felt more secure where I was. I was the first ever to get the Group Certificate in 1950, the first year it was introduced. We used to play some hurling across the road where Anthony Maher's house is now but because of the low numbers sport was not big at the time. When I was leaving in 1950 numbers were increasing as people became more aware of the value of education.

During the early 1940's, men brought the post by bicycle from Portlaoise to Clonaslee. The post for Tinnahinch Mountain was sorted at Gaffneys. The local postman was Bill Donnelly from Ballinalug and he delivered the post around Tinnahinch Mountain. Paddy Kavanagh on his bicycle continued on with the remaining post to the Clonaslee Post Office. Miss Guinan, who was Post Mistress until 1946, to be succeeded by Miss Cleary, then organised and sorted the post with the help of the two postmen, Tom Westman and Jim Fitzpatrick. Tom Westman was my godfather and Jim Fitzpatrick has two nephews Ned and Paddy Fitzpatrick living in Coolagh on the main Birr Road. Paddy Kavanagh who had brought the post by bicycle from Portlaoise also distributed the post around the village. He was replaced by Ted Laffey who had a motorcar and was contracted to bring it from Portlaoise later on. Jimmy Johnson worked for him and also did the post replacing Paddy Kavanagh.

At Christmas time the locals who always valued 'their' postmen would give them a tip of approximately half a crown or a drink. This could lead, as one can imagine, to the post arriving a bit late on those days. The postman bringing the post from Portlaoise began his round at the Railway Station in Mountmellick. He usually began at the house after the station. So he must have started his round around 6 am.

I went to my first county GAA match between Laois and Kildare in 1947 while I was still in school. It was a repeat of the Leinster Final in 1946. Laois won both games by two points. Graigecullen had a great team then and were County Champions. I missed my chance of carrying off Tommy Murphy in Tullamore after they won. I was up beside the group of supporters as they carried him shoulder high but I was in awe of him as he was a legend. That evening I met Jim Sweeney outside Adams, which his son Frank was to eventually own and call High Street House and he said Offaly will beat Laois in the next round. Instead Laois beat Offaly by twenty two points in Portlaoise in the Leinster Semi-Final. As it was to work out, Laois lost the Leinster Final to Meath by four points. That was the year that the prize was a trip to the Polo Grounds, New York for the All-Ireland Final and Laois was looking forward to being there but it was not to be.

To me there was never a Laois team like that. In 1946 they were beaten by Jimmy Murray's Roscommon in the All-Ireland Semi-Final. It was a controversial and dubious win. To this day it pains me. Kerry was an old team and I feel Laois could have been All-Ireland Champions. Why it pains me was the fact that Roscommon got two controversial goals while Laois were denied a goal when the Roscommon goalkeeper lay on the ball when it was over the line, while in the first half Roscommon got a goal that was very doubtful. And after all that Laois lost by only two points!

A group of us cycled to that game in Tullamore. In the group was Jim Young, James Young's grandfather, Jim Barrett, Matt and John 's father and Mick Barrett. We left the bikes in a cottage over the Railway Bridge beside Clonminch cemetery and walked into the town. We had sandwiches and lemonade in Lawler's yard, one of the most famous pubs in Tullamore and is now Spollens.

A minor game preceded the Kildare and Laois game. Paddy Dunne from Park was playing for Laois minors who later became a great Laois player at full back and centre back. He played on three Railway Cup winning teams with Leinster and was chosen on the Laois millennium team. The Laois players of that time were all heroes to me especially Tommy Murphy, Bill Delaney, Des Connolly and the captain Mick Aughney. Mickey Geraghty from

Kildare was my man of the match along with Boiler Whyte. I could write a book about them all. It was like as if they were fifteen Popes with the build-up they got from Micháel O'Hehir on the radio.

I finished in the Technical School in the summer of 1950. I worked for a time with farmers up and down and the going rate was three and sixpence per day. One of my memories of those years was being in the Parochial Hall on the May 31st 1948 when Father Doyle switched on the electric. We were the third village in the Republic to get electricity. Bansha in Tipperary, home of Muintir na Tire and Canon Hayes fame, was first and Rathvilly was the second village. They came from Rathvilly to Clonaslee to start the work in 1947. We were all mesmerised with this electricity. It cost thirty shillings per light for each room and some people could only afford one for the kitchen.

I went to work for Foynes', who were local builders in the building of the Health Centre and the Doctor's residence. I am the only one of those alive now. I finished working with Foynes at the building of Castlecuffe School. The principal of Castlecuffe School was Tom Honan, a Clare man and the assistant teacher who was known as a J.A.M. - Junior Assistant Mistress, was Carmel Honan from Baltinglass. They were involved in the local drama group producing plays in the hall. They got married in 1954 and moved back to his place in County Clare. A drama adjudicator, who came to Clonaslee for a drama production, said upon seeing Carmel Honan, that he didn't think he would see as good a looking girl in a country place. Bríd Malone was a very good actress in the local group as was Sean Mooney.

In October 1953 I went to work with Bord na Mona where I spent the next forty four years until I finished in 1997. I stopped on my birthday September 6th. On the same day Father Shortall died.

At the beginning I found Bord na Mona difficult. I cycled

one hundred and forty miles a week to and from work. I was expected to clock in at Boora yard in Ferbane parish at 8 am. Close by was the Power Station, which was being built when I started work. This Power Station has done its work and has now been levelled. The surrounding bog has been cut away, so our electricity is now coming from other stations. My first job was working at the building of the workshops in the yard. This lasted for three years. Mr Huggurt was the engineer. He was a Dublin man and stayed in Bolger's Hotel, Tullamore during the week. The general manager in Boora at the time was Louis Rattigan from Longford. Later he was to become Head Manager of Bord na Mona.

In 1954, contractors from Limerick installed the Water Treatment plant as you go up the mountain road by Peavoys at Gorrough. There were thirteen houses on the mile long road where the intake of the water was located. Not one family lives there now. Jim Rosney was the last to live there. This was a great boost as we had water on tap for the first time in the village.

I went up to the bog in 1956 to do shift work on the machines. I was on early shift and had to be there at six o'clock in the morning. I had to leave Clonaslee at 4.45 am. This meant rising at 4.15-4.30 am so I went to bed early the night before. The early shift ended at 2 pm. Every second week we alternated shifts with the late shift commencing at 2 pm and ending at 10 pm - eight-hour shifts. These shifts were in operation from mid-April to September. It was necessary to have a flash lamp on your bicycle in the early morning as you went to work. Conditions were bad at the time and goodwill was at a low ebb but it improved immensely as time went by.

When I was growing up there was a great Pipers band in Clonaslee. They used to play at Feis' and matches. On St Patrick's Day they played outside the Church after second Mass and marched from the chapel gate up to the Church of Ireland. Of course, there was no traffic to disrupt them in those days. They received many invitations to play at matches all over Laois and Offaly. They often played in Brady's field. Tom Brady was the owner before James Foynes. Tom Brady was a brother of Lar Brady who lived in Clonad and was chairman of the Laois GAA for over 40 years. They were a strong Republican family. Both Tom and Lar played football for Ballyroan. Lar was one of the longest serving Chairmen of the County Board. He was strict and fair. Tom Brady died in 1949-50 so that finished the GAA matches down there. The GAA then depended on the goodwill of farmers to give their fields for matches. Murphys from Kilmanman, gave a field for some matches opposite Kilmanman Cemetery.

Clonaslee and Clonad played a very tough match in 1945 in the Senior Hurling Championship at that venue. Clonad won that game. That year they had a super team. Big names on the Clonaslee team were Ned Troy, Mick Culleton of Brittas, Paddy Costelloe of Ballykaneen, Mick Kearney was another stalwart. He won a Junior Medal in 1933 and won his last Intermediate medal in 1955 playing for over twenty three years for the club. There were also other games in Casey's field in Coolnabanch and in Mathew's field in Bellair.

The pipers' band disbanded in 1948. Some band members played hurling as well. They paraded the teams, prior to a match, with the band and then took up the hurleys to play the game. One wonders how this tradition would be looked upon today. When Killoughey were playing Clonaslee in a tournament the Russell brothers, who were accomplished Offaly hurlers and in the pipe band, would find themselves marching with some of the Clonaslee opposition in the band.

Members of the band had different political affiliation and they often played at political rallies. This often led to tension and difference of opinion and some felt this was the reason they broke up. It was sad to see the band go as it had become part of the community and was known far and wide.

- Talking Memories -

2th October 1922 Transport and General Workers Union strike.
Farmers attempted to ban working threshing machines with a sign 'Up Labour' on it.
Bord na Mona prided itself on good labour relations however, there was a famous strike
in 1922. Photo of workers taken at farm in Cappasteen down the Tullamore Road.

Frank Dunne trained the band. He also trained bands in Mount Bolus and Killenard. He was known as a Pipe Major. He was in America for a while where he trained a band in Boston, Massachusettes which led the first Irish parade in that city. The Mount Bolus band played at his funeral.

Brittas Estate was divided in 1936 and the GAA acquired a field, which they still own, known as the Racecourse. Horse races were held there at the time Dunnes had the estate.

When I was growing up, that field in the evening time was full of young men practising hurling. There was no money at that time and it was the only pastime for young people. Mostly senior practice took place in that field along with juvenile games and school games. This was the home of the GAA for forty years. When the parish field, now known as Father Kehoe Park, became available all GAA activity moved down into the village. Clonaslee now play all their home league matches at this venue. Clonaslee's location bordering three Offaly parishes; Kinnitty, Kilcormac/Killoughey and Killeigh was not central enough for important championship matches. My greatest day following Clonaslee was when they won the Laois Senior Hurling Championship in 1975, captained by John O'Keeffe. They beat Clonad in the final and I was thrilled to be present. This was the third occasion for Clonaslee to win this Championship.

The burning of Brittas Castle and the draining of Lough Annagh were sad occasions in the life of Clonaslee. Lough Annagh had three hundred and fifteen acres under water. Two thirds of it was in Offaly and one third in Laois. It had a circumference of three miles and it was a brilliant feeding ground for roach and perch. We went down the Tullamore Road and turned left at Cush to get to the lake. It borders where the McCann family now live. It was drained in 1954 under the Brosna drainage scheme by the Board of Works. If it was now, there would be a lot of opposition from the local people. The Heritage and Sliabh Bloom Association would get involved also. It was a beautiful lake with great fishing ground and it really was a big tourist loss to the area. Each Sunday saw many people going down to the lake to fish while parents often had a picnic on Mohan's Strand bordering the lake.

When I was growing up, the present GAA pitch was known as Father Murray's fields. There were small fields, three separated by hedges and in the centre was the small ruin of an abandoned house. Water was pumped by hand from the pump for the few horses and a cow. In Father Keogh's time the hedges were removed and it was turned into a large sports field. The official opening was the summer of 1980. Laois played Wexford in hurling and Fermanagh in football. After that it was called Father Keogh Park.

During the course of my work in Boora I met many men who represented Offaly in hurling and football. I found Offaly people very friendly much the same as Laois people. The river boundary makes no difference on the human level. There was plenty of banter before a Laois/Offaly game. I worked with Joe Murphy from Kilcormac who represented Offaly for ten years at corner back. I often got a haircut in Noel McGees, Tullamore. He was the only man who had the distinction of captaining Offaly in both football and hurling. Some of the greatest games I attended were the Inter Bord na Mona Works Championship. Great rivalry existed between Derrygreenagh, Boora, Clonsast, Mount Dillon and Killenthomas in Kildare. Each team had quite a few countymen.

Joe Young in Derry Grogan's farmyard, Kilcormac, in front of his car with his tractor in the background.

I married a girl from Offaly in 1968, Frances Doyle and I lived for a few years in Kilcormac before coming to live in Chapel

Street. We inherited a farm in Killoughey in 1975. I have seen many changes in Clonaslee over the years with many generations coming and going. When I came to Clonaslee the old bridge at the entrance to the town was being demolished. It was an old hump back bridge similar to ones all over Ireland. These bridges had one benefit, they slowed down the traffic. The River Clodiagh flows by my front door and as the poem says *"Men may come and men may go but I go on forever"*.

Eilish Maher

We Have the New Look Today

EILISH MAHER, MAIN STREET

I am a native of Clontyglass, Portlaoise. It is a townsland in the parish of Ballyfin. As far as I know Ballyfin parish has now become part of Mountrath parish. I went to school in Barnashrone National School about a mile from home. In those days we all walked to school. There were two teachers, Mrs Phelan who cycled out daily from Derrycloney in Mountmellick and Miss Breen who also cycled out from Mountmellick. The school is still there and I know they now have an extra room. When I was there the numbers on the roll book were about fifty. This has now increased. The only games we played in the school were tíg, hopscotch, and marbles. As it was a rural school all of us pupils, on going home from school, would help on the land. We were all sons and daughters of farmers. Because of this we were very conscious of the four seasons; saving the turf, bringing home the hay and in September/October the threshing. We cut our turf in a bog that spanned four townslands: Clontyglass, Barnashrone, Clontowra and Cloneygowan. My father lived in Clontyglass, my grandfather lived in Clontowra and he inherited his farm from an aunt and uncle. The bog is now cut away. It was drained and is now grassland and forestry.

One thing I remember from my school days is that every family brought a penny to the school every Monday morning. This was used to provide cocoa which the teachers made for us on an open fire and we drank it with our lunch at 12:30 each day.

Ballyfin was considered to be a very rural parish. In my time Ballyfin College was staffed by the Patrician Brothers. The school was sold and it is now known worldwide as a five star luxurious hotel.

After leaving the primary school, where in the final year, every pupil was obliged to sit an exam in English, Irish and Maths known as the Primary Certificate, I went to Ballymahon Secondary School. The reason I went there was that I had an aunt teaching in the primary school. She was a sister of my father, known as Sister Clement, a Mercy nun. My cousins, the Fitzpatricks from Esker, Ballyfin also went to Ballymahon Secondary School as did my sisters Maura, Teresa, Frances and Breda. We saw our aunt Sister Clement the day we arrived and the day we left for Christmas, Easter and summer holidays. Usually we brought home a letter from her to members of our family.

My time in Ballymahon was during the war years. I can well remember Sister Mercedes coming in at study to tell us the war was over. We all cheered thinking that the "rations" were also over. Travel was difficult in those years. That is why we never went or mixed with other schools for games as petrol was scarce and rationed. What a pleasant contrast for school pupils today as we are hoping that Clonaslee College will win the double in the basketball finals in the National Basketball Arena in Tallaght.

Outside the Post Office. L-R Seamus Foynes, Maura Lalor, Paddy Bates, Dinny Kelly, Breda Lalor.

In my final year in Ballymahon I was due to sit the Civil Service Entrance Exam in Athlone. The day before the exam I got the mumps. I was put into a separate bedroom and isolated for a few days. There were no antibiotics available at that time. After I did the Leaving Certificate I did a crash course in shorthand, typing and accounts. I did the course in Dublin, there was no course available locally and I stayed with an aunt during the three months. The school sent me for an interview to Briscoe, Smith and Co. where one of the tests was to type out a balance sheet and a business letter. And so I got my first job with them in 1949. Dublin was a quiet city back then. What was known as the *'new look'*, the first new fashion designs after the Second World War had come into vogue. Out of my wages I managed to put by enough money every week to buy a *'new look'* coat. This was a coat that flared out from the waist to the ankles and was all the go.

One day my sister Maura who was a trainee nurse in Sir Patrick Dunne's Hospital, her friend Breda O'Sullivan from Bansha, Co Tipperary also a trainee nurse and myself were walking down Moore Street when one of the famous stall women shouted across the street to another stall holder *"We have the 'new look' today"*. Being country girls we did not know what to think or how to take it. So we quietly turned around and went back to Henry Street.

In early 1950 I sat an exam with Laois County Council in the Courthouse, Portlaoise. The County Council had their offices there then. Later I was called for an interview. My father had died suddenly and I remember going into the interview dressed in black. That was the custom at the time. One was expected to dress for a year in black while men wore a black diamond shaped patch on the arm of their coat which was stitched on. I was interviewed by the County Manager M.H. Veale along with the acting County Secretary and a third person from Offaly County Council. Laois and Offaly County Councils were all one at that time. After a medical examination, which was compulsory, I was appointed to the Law Agents Office of the County Council. The daily work involved purchase of land for the County Council houses and road widening. Little did I know I was to meet Kathleen Lettice Youell who was selling land in Bonastick, Clonaslee. I also met Jim and Jack Foynes coming in to sign a contract to build houses in

Clonaslee. I remember Kathleen Lettice Youell drove a three wheel car. It had one wheel on the front and two wheels behind. It was a small, low car. I was there from August 1950 to 1958 when I got married. I had to leave then because of the Marriage Ban. Unlike now, when you can continue working, the employment rules of that era obliged one to retire. One of my aunts told me, *"Do you know what you are doing? You are leaving a permanent pensionable job to get married"*.

Eilish and Michael Maher on their wedding day September 29th 1958 with Father Jim Kaye.

I met my husband at Father Brown's Whist Drive which was run in aid of the building of the new church in Portlaoise. The Whist Drive was a yearly event held in St Fintan's Hospital. I came to live with my husband, Michael Maher in Clonaslee on November 1st 1958. I was married the previous September in Ballyfin Church. The Parish Priest at the time was Father Con Phelan. He was a keen hurling follower and was known to have a sweet tooth.

My husband was originally from Rathleague, Portlaoise and at that time he worked in the office of the Leinster Express. He was appointed Post Master in Clonaslee, filling the vacancy left by Dermot Connolly who moved to Abbeyleix. His son is now Postmaster there. Prior to him Mrs Kavanagh was the Post Mistress. Mrs Kavanagh's husband bought a pub in Wexford and they moved down there. Before her there was a Miss Guinan who reared cattle. The story goes that she would put her dog to mind the counter when she went to look at the cattle. The dog had a reputation of being a good guard dog, so the Post Office was safe.

We got the job after doing an interview in Portlaoise. Mr M Darcy conducted the interview. He was head Postmaster in Portlaoise. He was happy I was able to speak and understand Irish.

We had to buy the premises from the previous postmaster. This was an advantage as the post equipment such as the telephone switch board, the public telephone kiosk and the letter sorting facilities - the little pigeon holes - were all there.

Only four people had phones, the Parish Priest, the local Doctor, the Garda Barracks, and James Daly who was the District Court Clerk. There was a fifth phone - the kiosk in the Post Office for public use.

On the front wall of our premises outside on the street was the following title:

CLONASLEE MONEY ORDER OFFICE
PARCEL POST
TELEGRAMS
STAMPS
POSTAL ORDERS
REGISTERED POST
LATEST TIME FOR POSTING 5:30 PM.

The letters and parcels each day came to Mountmellick Post Office. There, they were sorted and Clonaslee post usually arrived around 7 am to 8 am. A private contractor from Portlaoise had that job. The driver's name was Michael Rodgers. It was re-sorted in Clonaslee by the postmen and ourselves and then delivered. The first postmen we knew in Clonaslee when we arrived were Jack Comerford from Capparogan and Tom Westman, Tullamore Road. They started their rounds on their bicycles around nine o'clock. They brought back letters in the evening for posting. They had to be in by 5.30 pm as it is today. Christmas was the busiest time. An awful lot of parcels had to be delivered, with many being sent to England. Turkeys were sent to England. They had to be wrapped in cloth and fine sacking with a special customs label. The reason for this was that people had no fridges so the turkeys were stitched into this wrapping. Turkeys were scarce in England which is hard to imagine nowadays.

My main job was to work the switchboard. People came in every day, mainly to make calls to Portlaoise Hospital as well as business calls. This could be tedious for the caller as the one line into the hospital could be busy with other calls. And so the person would have to wait a long time. All the local numbers were in single digits. Our number was Clonaslee 2.

It cost a $2\ ^1/_2$ penny stamp to post a letter. We had stamps ranging from a half penny up to one Irish Pound. If I had kept one of each of those stamps they would now be very valuable. A philatelist, a stamp collector usually bought four stamps with the stamp edge on them and put them into a collector's book. Lovely stamps have been issued over the years by the G.P.O. in Dublin. It's too late now to start collecting.

There was a shop on the same floor as the Post Office, selling tobacco, loose sweets, which you had to weigh up, along with biscuits and other small items. H.B. ice cream had a depot in Tullamore. They supplied the fridge and we began selling blocks of ice cream, vanilla or ripple. We sold them in two penny, four penny and six penny wafers. I remember a man saying recently to me that if you had one shilling you could buy a six penny ice cream over an inch thick, a four penny Cadbury plain chocolate bar which would cost a euro today and still have two pennies left to buy sweets or penny bars.

When Joe Conroy who owned a pub and grocery retired across the road from us, we applied for a news agency. We were successful. I remember going over to buy flour and some groceries from Joe Conroy. He filled a glass of wine and gave it to me to celebrate the birth of our son. I said, *"I don't drink alcohol"*. He said, *"Go on, it's good for you, it's only tonic wine, Buckfast, made by the monks."* At that time, women did not drink in Public Houses so I drank the wine in a few mouthfuls, as fast as I could so as not to be seen drinking. Coming across the street I stepped high as I thought the street was coming up to meet me. Looking back one can see how times have changed.

Computerisation of Clonaslee Post Office.
Eilish Maher attending Eileen Daly and Marie Keating.

Gradually we extended the shop and the house which we re-roofed. We replaced the flag floors. We began to sell some children's clothes, shirts, socks and pants. As we were using an upstairs bedroom for storage we built storage space out the back.

We had to man the switch board twenty four hours a day as more people got phones. Many girls who had done their Junior Certificate and were hoping to become nurses came to us looking for employment. They could not apply for nursing until they were eighteen so they had two years to spare. Some left after the two years and went to bigger post offices such as Portarlington, Mountmellick, and Stradbally. The first girl we had was Patricia Conroy of Reary. She stayed with us. Later on she became Post Mistress in an office in County Kildare. Sean and Denise Flynn took over the Post Office from us on February 2nd 2004.

Eilish Maher with her successor Sean Flynn outside the Post Office.

Pounds, shillings and pence was the currency until the 15th February 1971 which made the counting of stamps, postal orders, saving stamps and cash very tedious and time consuming. This had to be done once a week and recorded for unannounced inspections by the head Postmaster and his assistant. The 1st of January 2002 was a very memorable day being the day of the changeover to the present day Euro currency. Some of the people did not trust the decimal conversion. On one occasion a customer remarked *"I'm not shopping here anymore, I'll go where they are dealing in the old money."* Needless to say after about two weeks they understood the working of the new currency.

The postal system within the Post Office was computerised in 1992. A man came out from Portlaoise at lunch time that day, 1 pm to 2 pm, and showed us how to start the computer, pay the pensions and do Post Office deposits and withdrawals. It was a real crash course. If we ran into difficulties we were given a special number to ring. It was by mistakes that we quickly adapted to the new system.

Michael Dunne

Macra was a University

MICHAEL DUNNE, BALLYMACRORY

When I was going to school there were big wrought iron gates at the entrance to Brittas Avenue. At present you can see one pier next to the gate lodge where Edmund Dunne now lives. His mother Lil, was in her nineties when she passed away. There was one small gate at each side, which pedestrians used. Clonaslee grew up around the trade and commerce of the Brittas Estate. The Dunnes were the landlords of all Clonaslee.

They owned thousands of acres extending as far as Mountrath. The castle was burned in 1942 and the Land Commission divided it in 1945. Adjacent to the main entrance to Brittas was a hump back bridge over the Clodiagh River.

This bridge was part of the Main Street at the west end of the village. On Sundays it was the meeting place for all and sundry as the locals sat on the bridge telling stories and exchanging the happenings of the past week. As the country became more mechanised with cars and tractors the bridge was deemed dangerous. This I well know from personal experience. One day while turning down the Tullamore Road with a load of cattle, the tractor and trailer overturned and Donal Conroy and myself had a lucky escape. The County Council removed it and built a new bridge in the early 1970's. At the time its removal was not mourned but later on people began to miss the old bridge, as it had become the social and gathering place of the village. The old bridge cost many a person a new sump in their car when they came down the bridge too fast and hit the street in front of John Moran's Garage.

In my school days, rural electrification came to Clonaslee. That changed the life for the village and the countryside. It arrived in Clonaslee in 1948 but it did not get out to my part of the parish until 1961 - Ballymacrory. In the winter days we all went down to school, about two miles, by pony and trap. In the summer we walked. In the summer time we lazed, going along wondering at nature, taking in the butterflies and trying to distinguish the various birds. We all found our own birds nests keeping it a secret, as we thought, from each other. There was no need to rush home then, as we had no play stations or computer games. Looking back they appear to have been good times and we always had a healthy dinner when we arrived home from school.

My father died in 1950. My mother and our uncle carried on the farm. My uncle was also a blacksmith. In my young days I spent a lot of time blowing the bellows in the forge. The forge was across the yard. Neighbours came and got their horses shod and their machinery repaired. He got his iron from P. & H. Egan at the local branch and also the coal for the fire. Part of my work and any young chap that came in was blowing the bellows. The only payment was the enjoyment and the knowledge one received at seeing jobs being completed. One learned how horses were shod and what amazed all was why they never kicked when the nails went into their hooves. Payment was made when the harvest came in or cattle were sold. We also saw horse carts being made and wheels being bound at the big fire around the binding stone. The wheel was laid on the binding stone and the hot iron band was then placed down over it and cooled quickly with water so as not to let it burn the fellows - the outer timber of the wheel.

At the threshing.

Farm horses and the forge disappeared in the 1950's when tractors and modern farm equipment came on the scene.

My brother Pat and myself are still farming. In our time we did a bit of everything; corn, beet and cattle. In later years we went into dairying. We have now retired from that. Over the years farming has changed enormously since we joined the E.E.C. I always thought it was the way forward and I remember going to many meetings where the issue was debated.

A Vocational School was built in Clonaslee in 1937. When I was going in the 1950's there were only six pupils in First Year, five girls and myself. We had a wonderful headmaster in Mr P.D. Brickley. He came from Clonakilty in West Cork. After leaving the Vocational School I joined Macra na Feirme, which had been set up by P.D. Brickley in the 1940's. P.D. Brickley was able to get top class speakers to lecture on various topics. On one occasion he engaged a speaker from the Canadian Embassy who spoke to us about life in Canada and its many opportunities. This was my main social outlet. We took part in public speaking competitions and questions times. We had an annual social in the school and we used to have an annual outing where we visited a well-run farm, which benefited us on our own farm. It was a great organisation and gave us a great training in leadership. Macra ran leadership courses from time to time consisting of setting up and running meetings. Really Macra was a University for us as we received higher levels of education. Later on, I became secretary of Macra.

The I.C.A. secretary at that time was the late Maureen Brophy. She lived in the townsland of Boyle. Her daughter Bríd married Tommy Kelly and now lives opposite Kilmanman cemetery. Tommy, along with Dinny Kelly, now take care of Kilmanman cemetery. Both Bríd and I were elected joint secretaries of the Clonaslee Produce and Livestock Show which was a big annual event and required a lot of work. It was very successful. It is still going strong and is now known as the Clonaslee Show. I also got involved in other local activities. I was a founder member of the Clonaslee Pig Co-operative Society, which was of great benefit to local pig breeders. It was later taken over by Avonmore. For over twenty years I was a committee member of the local Parochial Hall where a Whist Drive was held every Sunday night.

Michael Dunne in the Holy Land with Jerusalem in the background

Following a meeting of the hall committee the late Father Kehoe, Parish Priest, suggested that we form a community council. He had seen one and had been observing how other parishes were developing and felt this would be an asset in our local community. In 1972 an election was held in the parish to elect members to the council. It was duly formed and I was elected its first Chairman. Our first big project saw us liasing with Laois County Council to set up a Group Water Scheme in the west of the parish. The water scheme brought great benefits to the people up the Birr Road including Castlecuffe. We also started the Old Folks Party, which continues to this day.

In the early 1980's a new Community Council under the chairmanship of Donal Sweeney was set up. We bought a site and in 1988 a foundation stone was laid for a new community centre. It is still going great. It has helped to foster a great community spirit in our area. Many visitors from bigger centres are envious of our achievements. A local lotto was formed to raise funds for the community centre. I am still a promoter and the Community Centre's debt is fully cleared. Even with inflation the Centre is still managing to keep its head above water.

Chris Horan and Michael Dunne at digging of the foundation for the Vocational School now Clonaslee College.

One thing that gave me great satisfaction was the organising of the Dunne Clan Reunion. Other families were having Clan gatherings and this prompted me to bring the Dunnes together. We had a successful banquet with about two hundred and fifty people attending. People from America, Canada and England came. It took place in the Community Centre in June 2000. The reunion was spread over one weekend. We visited the Dunne Castles and other historical sites. There were talks and film shows by Harry Dunne from Florida. Joe Dunne who wrote the book *'Dunne People and Places'* gave a presentation.

We also launched Joe McCabe's book. Joe McCabe or Seosamh MacCába was born in the village of Clonaslee in 1881 and lived where Paddy Farrell lives now on Chapel Street. He trained as a teacher and taught in Moneenroe, Castlecomer. Later on he was appointed Principal of Clonad National School, Portlaoise where he worked from 1907 to 1948. His mother's maiden name was Dunne. Seosamh (Joe) compiled *"Historical Notes on Laois and Place Names of Ballyroan"* which was published by the Old Laois Society. He then went on to write *"Dú thaí Uí Riagáin"*, a history of Uí Riagáin territory and a genealogy of its chieftains - the O'Dunnes. It is hoped and planned that these reunions will continue.

At fifty eight years of age I suffered heart illness requiring surgery. Later I got rheumatoid arthritis and am now wheelchair bound, but I can still look back over the years with great satisfaction.

Michael Dunne and his faithful friend

Desmond Dillon

Penny Farthing Bike

DESMOND DILLON, MAIN STREET

I came to Clonaslee in 1938. I was born in 1914 so I was twenty four years of age. I took up the position in the Vocational school as Woodwork teacher and allied subjects Mechanical Drawing and Maths. I went to the Metropolitan School of Art between the National Library and the Dail in Dublin. George Atkinson was the Principal in the School of Art at the time. The man in charge of my course was a C.J. O'Connor. He was appointed by the Department of Education to run the teachers course.

In Dublin I stayed in digs in Mount Street. My landlady's name was Mrs Conway, a Dublin woman. There were two pals in the same course as me staying there. Colm O'Connor, a Kerryman and the other was Pat Murray, a Waterford man. Up to recently I kept in touch with both of them. Colm O'Connor, after qualifying, went to teach in Carlow Vocational School and Pat Murray went to teach in his own county Waterford. There were twenty of us altogether in the scholarship offered by the Department of Education.

My father, Philip Dillon, a Limerick man from 2 Lower Mallow Street in the city, off O'Connell Street facing down to the Shannon, was a woodwork teacher in Portlaoise Technical School. He had been with the Congested District Board under the British in the West of Ireland and Donegal. This was a Board set up to give employment and my father was an instructor with them teaching crafts, art and building skills. He applied to the committee in County Laois for a vacancy in the Technical School, so from there my father developed a love of timber and I used to attend night classes given by my father in Portlaoise. I won prizes in shows like Rathdowney in woodwork when I was young. I never found Dublin intimidating as I used to go on holidays to my Aunt who lived in Clontarf, a sister of my mother.

Portlaoise, when I was in school there, was known as Maryborough named after Queen Mary. The remains of the old walled town were still there down along by the Christian Brothers School known as Tower Hill. Odlums had a flourmill in that part of the town. At that time it was worked by a millrace, which the water from the river Triog powered. There was no electricity in Portlaoise then. The Railway Station played an important part in the town's commerce, the G.S.R. - Great Southern Railway, puffing regularly and emitting a frequent hoot as it came through. There was a big goods depot at Conneyborough where we often went down to play.

L-R: Des and Maureen Dillon, Frank Boyle, Engineer for the local water scheme and Mary Margaret O'Mahony in 1954.

My course in the School of Art lasted two years. I was there in 1932 when the Eucharistic Congress was held. The Phoenix Park was full of people from all over Ireland. The Park was never as full of people again until the visit of Pope John Paul II. During my stay in Dublin I had an opportunity to visit the shows in the Theatre Royal, Hawkins Street and the Queens Theatre in Pearse Street. It used to be gas in the Queens, listening to the people in the 'gods' making wise-cracks about the performance. I often visited the Abbey Theatre whenever there was a good play on. I remember being at *'Juno and the Paycock', 'Riders to the Sea',* and *'The Plough and the Stars'. 'Juno and the Paycock'* made a big impression on me at the time. The most enjoyable feature in the Theatre Royal was when the organ was played before a show or film. It came up through the stage from the pit below. I also visited the Capital Theatre near the GPO along with an occasional visit to the Gate Theatre beside the Rotunda. I remember the Capital Theatre because there was a restaurant upstairs.

Every St Patrick's Day, Pat Brickley, the Principal in the school here in Clonaslee, went to the Railway Cup Finals in Croke Park. This was a competition between the four provinces and it was considered a great honour to be selected on the Leinster team. After the matches we always had a good Irish stew or bacon and cabbage in the Capital Restaurant. We usually went up and back from Dublin by rail.

When I arrived in Clonaslee in September 1938, I stayed with Mr and Mrs Tom O'Rourke of Bonastick. I felt at home on my arrival and I had a pal with me John Cusack, who stayed in O'Rourkes and we shared a room. He was in charge of the shop run by the Tullamore Co-operative which was the town side of the Vocational School. Evelyn Cusack, the lady who presents the weather chart on RTE is the daughter of John Cusack. Evelyn was born in Clonaslee and her mother was a Leahy from Cadamstown. The family lived in Chapel Street where Joe and Babs Young now live.

I met Pat Brickley for the first time on the opening day of the school term. There was one more teacher, Miss Meaney, who was the Domestic Science teacher. Miss Meaney was later to leave Clonaslee and go to Carlow. The Vocational School had been officially opened the year before in 1938, by the Minister of Education, Tom Derrigh. Pat Brickley was named the first Principal. Pat Brickley hailed from Clonakilty and trained in Glasnevin, Dublin at the Botanical Gardens in Rural Science. On meeting him little did I realise that our lives together would play a significant part in the general education of the area. We worked together in the school for forty two years retiring around 1980. The first year that I was here the numbers in the school ranged between forty and sixty, this included those taking night classes.

My subjects were general woodwork which included craft and building trade. This extended to roofing and everything relating to house building. Night classes related to the making of chairs, tables, and house furnishing. Night classes were from 7 pm to 10 pm. Day classes from 9.30 am to 4 pm. During the day classes I also taught mechanical drawing and maths allied subjects to woodwork. The Department of Education had an exam called the Group Certificate. Students sat for this exam usually after three years in the school. There were also exams for girls in Domestic Science and Scholarships. It was hard to keep up the numbers in the school so we had to go around canvassing. Pat Brickley and I visited all the National Schools in the catchment area recruiting pupils for the school. We also visited the parents of the parish in their homes. There was a real danger of the school closing unless we could maintain the numbers. It became very serious when Pat Brickley had to go back to the Army during the emergency. He was recalled to the army as he had been a member when he was studying in Glasnevin. So he was away for six months in 1940 and a graduate from UCD in Botany and Rural Science replaced him.

Another part of my work was afternoon and night classes in the surrounding areas. I taught general woodwork in Cadamstown, Mountmellick, Rosenallis, Clonaghadoo, Ballyfin and Clonaheen. These classes were held in the local hall or the National School. I did these two nights a week. I cycled there and back getting home around 11 pm. This helped in our recruitment drive for the school, as it was an opportunity to meet prospective children and their parents.

One night coming back from Clonaghadoo, I thought I saw somebody else or a figure going along on top of the hedge in the light of a lamp. I jumped off the bike and stopped with the fright. I was coming up between Drummond and Reary Valley. I couldn't make it out and bolted home when I got my breath back. Shortly afterwards I saw a man coming into the village on a Penny Farthing bike, I solved the mystery. I realised that what I saw on the Reary Valley road was not an apparition but this man sitting up high on his Penny Farthing bike.

On the way to O'Moore Park in 1959
L-R: Willy Dillon, Billy Morrissey, Philip Dillon, Des Dillon
with Laois supporters in the background.

When the Vocational School began to cater for new subjects, Clonaslee pupils began to sit for the Intermediate and Leaving Certificates. As the staff needed to grow, extra teachers were employed. This meant more classrooms and pre-fabs were erected behind the school. Around this time I became Vice-Principal. I received a small increase in salary for extra duties such as looking after enrolment and library duties. I must say I enjoyed my life teaching and it was very gratifying when pupils came back to thank me for my interest in them and their success. One of the things I was most proud of was when I completed a table or art box made up of veneers or different timbers and there was not a single nail or screw used in its construction. One of my former pupils, Pat Byrne gained first place in Group Certificate Maths in Ireland. His mother was the last teacher in Tinnahinch School. At one stage I was games master and brought the pupils out to play hurling and football. In the winter the pupils played chess, draughts and cards in the school.

L-R: Mary Margaret and Tim O'Mahoney, Billy Morrissey, Des and Maureen Dillon in 1956.

Where I live now was formerly a drapers shop. As you can see the name Morrisey is over the door. My wife's father was a Wexford man from Bunclody. Formerly he worked in Scallys of Tullamore. It is now closed. When I got married first I lived in rented accommodation in a house on the estate of Brittas Castle. When we came down to live in the village we lived beside Brickleys where Foynes live now. Then Maureen and I bought the house next door to Morriseys, which had come up for auction. It was convenient as Maureen could look after her mother when her father died.

When I retired I drew plans and designs for houses and

extensions. I began to map out sites for private houses and submit them to the local County Council. I enjoyed this work because I was used to design and art at school in Dublin so it was a great chance to get involved again. Schools commissioned me to design annual awards for Student of the Year and Sports Star of the Year.

Des Dillon and his wife Maureen with a Christmas turkey

The closing of P & H Egans along with Williams changed the appearance of the village. Also the closing of the Church of Ireland and Mrs Webster's school was significant. I will be ninety three on October 5th 2007.

Life is full of surprises. When I was going up to Dublin to arrive at the School of Art for the first time, I saw this soldier on duty in his sentry box beside the Dail. His face seemed familiar so I went over to get a better view of him and it turned out he had been a school pal from Portlaoise. His surname was Cummins and he was now in the Army. We had a great chat about our schooldays and about our present circumstances. We also discussed the politics of the time. If I had to ask him, maybe I could have gone in to hear the T.D.'s in the Dail and maybe meet Eamon DeValera or Liam Cosgrave.

Annie O'Donovan

Up the Glen

ANNIE O'DONOVAN, MAIN STREET

I was born in the big glen of Glenties, Co Donegal. When I was born there were hills on both sides with a river flowing down the middle. When you went up a hill you went down the far side into a glen and as there were many hills and glens the area became known as Glenties. The river was named Owenea and flowed into the sea at Ardara. When you left Sligo you passed through Bundoran, Donegal Town and on to Ardara and then

Glenties. For those who don't know it Ardara is a fine big town similar in size to Mountmellick.

Our house was about a mile out from the village of Glenties. It was called Buncrobog. It is an Irish name and translated it means *'the bottom of the basket'.* My father was a farmer living on a small acreage and reared sheep on the mountainside. I had one sister called Mary who was older than me. We both went to the local school in Buncrobog, which was right beside us. The Master's name was James McLoone. He had a brother Fr Arthur McLoone who was a teacher in St Eunan's College in Letterkenny. It was a two-teacher school. The other teacher was Bella Gallagher. The Master was a great teacher. When I left off to go to boarding school in Falcarragh I had enough Algebra done to sit my Inter Certificate. He was a local man from Glenties, married and cycled out to the school every day. If you were interested in progressing and getting on he would lay out work for you every night.

My sister Mary was not as keen as I was in studying but she was great with her hands. She was great at knitting. When Mary finished primary school she spent two years with my father on the land and then went into McDevitts Knitting Factory. The two McDevitt brothers, Paddy and Jim were remarkable men. At one time they had four hundred employed in the factory. This was in 1928. They manufactured all woolen clothes, jumpers, cardigans, socks, etc. This was a great industry for Glenties as it meant employment for everybody. Also the local farmers were sure of a market for their wool. When the two brothers came to retire they left most of their money to the people of Glenties. They set up the McDevitt Institute in an old house in the town, which they bought and renovated. This became the local Vocational School funded by the McDevitts. It is no longer in existence for when the money ran out there was nobody to put more money into the project. They also paid a local nurse to visit the homes of the elderly, something similar to 'carers' of today, so they were before their time.

They handed over the factory to a nephew and a niece but within two years the whole enterprise closed down due to lack of management experience.

During my sister Mary's time she worked her way up to be one of the designers of the Fair Isle Jumper. These jumpers had an individual design on the front and were exported to America and all over the world. If you pass through Glenties you can still see the McDevitt Factories, one on either side of the street.

I spent four years in Coláiste Bhríde in Falcarragh doing my Intermediate Certificate and Leaving Certificate. The school was run by the Loreto nuns who tried to make ladies out of us. Looking back discipline was strict in the school. One had to be on time, punctuality was emphasized. All subjects with the exception of English were taught through Irish and I must say I got a great love for the Irish language. There were a hundred boarders, no day pupils and the food was great! I look back on those years with fondness even though one would be lonely, as we were allowed no visitors during the term. From there I got a good Leaving Certificate entitling me to my place in Carysfort Training College for Primary Teachers.

When in the Primary School, I made friends with the Breslins, the Gallaghers and the Sweeneys, all Donegal local people. On a wet day when we got to school the Master made us stand around the turf fire in the room and all you could see was steam going up from our clothes. There was always a good fire and when he thought your clothes were dry you went back to your desk.

In Secondary School during the four years I made friends with Margaret Leydon, from Mayo; Kathleen Burke from Galway and Brid McHugh from Donegal. The three of them accompanied me to Carysfort Training College. Over the years I lost contact with them.

I spent two years in Carysfort. I will remember the last Sunday before I left Falcarragh for Carysfort, the Reverend Mother addressing us for the final time. Her words stood out in my memory as she said *'I am sorry you are leaving our jurisdiction, the Loreta Nuns, to go under the Mercy Nuns'*. The implication being that they regarded their training of us to be unrivalled.

I left Glenties by train - there is no train now in Glenties, so much for so called progress - for Strabane and on to Dublin in September 1937. I went on my own and other girls joined me en route heading for Carysfort. In Amiens Street Station there was great bustle and we got the tram from O'Connell Street out to Blackrock and the Training College. There were about fifty girls, from all over Ireland, in my class. There were also nuns from different congregations doing their training. It was certainly different from Falcarragh with more freedom and less restriction. It was up to yourself to work and get your exams. One of the first things I noticed was the different pronunciation of the Irish language by the girls from Connacht and Munster. In Donegal the word for bread was pronounced *'aran'* while Connacht and Munster seemed to pronounce it *'arán'* making the word sound longer. In Falcarragh we spoke Irish all the time while in Dublin we spoke English. This gave those of us from Donegal an advantage in Irish exams. An amazing thing was that the girls who came from the Fíor Ghaeltacht - Irish speaking area - failed their bi-lingual Certificate exam because their grammar was bad while the rest of us passed it.

I didn't see an awful lot of Dublin as we only got out on a Saturday from 9 am - 1 pm. The train fare into Dublin was five pence and we all preferred to go down to Blackrock and have a cup of tea and a scone than use it going into the city. When I did go in it was usually to get books in Easons on O'Connell Street. Nelson's Pillar dominated the street then. Christmas and Easter we were allowed home. In June 1939 I qualified as a National Teacher.

In September of that year the Second World War started and England was planning to evacuate children to Ireland. The plan was principal teachers in country schools were requested to go around and see how many houses could take children. The graduates of that year were called in to replace those teachers. And so I found myself going to Mohill in Co Leitrim where I spent two months.

From there I went to Dunreigh Fort situated on the coast of Donegal. Formerly there was a military barracks occupied by the English Army. When I went the Irish Army occupied the Fort. The children of the soldiers came to the school. There were two schools at that time, one for the boys and another for the girls. I spent six weeks filling in for the Principal. When the English occupied the Fort they brought their children to school in the morning along with two hampers of sandwiches, one for the children and a small one for the teachers. When the Irish soldiers came there were no hampers.

In 1940 I got a permanent appointment in the Girls Convent School in Carndonagh. It was in the north of the county, near Malin Head and over sixty miles from home. It was staffed by the Mercy nuns and it was a four room school. Carndonagh is a fine town as big as Tullamore at that time and I stayed with Mrs. Doherty and her family outside the town. I was teaching Fifth Class and I had around twenty five girls in the class. I was to spend three years there until 1944. It was during the war and we often went into Derry to get white bread. At that time the American Army were in Derry. When the British Army was on parade they marched down the Main Street known as The Strand, eyes looking straight ahead. The Americans would march with eyes looking to right and left saluting the girls as they went by. They would also throw small money on the side of the street to see the children fighting for it. As far as we were concerned they had little or no training and we all commented '*America how are you*'.

It was in Cardonagh that I met my future husband Tadgh O'Donovan. He was a chemist and was managing a pharmacy where the owner had died. He was a Cork man from Donoughmore near Macroon. We got married in January 1944. The Parish Priest Canon Forker was very old and so the Chaplain I had in Falcarragh School, Father Danny Molloy, married us in the church at Edeninfagh, which was in the parish of Glenties. So you probably are wondering how I ended up in Co Laois?

The Chemist Shop, 58 Main Street, Portlaoise.

When Tadgh was going to Dublin as a student he always went by bus, which passed through Portlaoise. On each occasion, once a month, he noticed a house, which was vacant and had a 'For Sale' sign up. Nobody seemed to want it.

So when he ended his term in November working in Cardonagh, he went to Portlaoise and rented this house, 58 Main

Street, for two guineas a week. Previous to that it had been a draper's shop. Every time Tadgh went to the bank to pay the two guineas the manager would come out and say *'Would you not think of buying that place'*, making us believe that the bank might own it. A year later we did buy it paying £150 for the whole property. It was a two storey building with three bedrooms and a large shop. Off the shop was a dining room. Upstairs along with the three bedrooms was a sitting room that had a magnificent fireplace, all marble in different shades. Beside the fireplace in the wall was a bell which could ring down to the kitchen indicating that in times past people of substance must have occupied the house.

So Tadhg and I came to live in Portlaoise in January 1944. It was during the war and where there was just two of us in the house rationing was dire. Butter was so scarce, each person being allowed two ounces. The same with sugar but since I did not use sugar Tadgh had four ounces a week. There was no white bread, only brown and it was awful. Tea was also very scarce but when Tadgh was leaving Carndonagh somebody gave him a present of a half chest of tea which had come over the border from Derry. This lasted us a good few years as we still collected our two ounces every week.

On arriving in Portlaoise we knew no one. It appeared to us as a dead town. Carndonagh, which we had left, was booming because of its proximity to the border and as well the smuggling of short commodities meant there was plenty of money in circulation. It appeared to us as a very quiet area with very few cars as petrol was rationed. Hardly any family had a car, it was all bicycles. Buses came through the town as it was on the main Dublin - Cork route. The Railway Line also came through the town. Portlaoise, being so quiet, it was easy to hear the whistle of the railway engines as they gave off steam.

There were three chemist shops in the town and here we were about to set up a fourth. Three elderly men were running the other pharmacies so we felt we were not that welcome as we were now in competition. We opened at the top of the town, four shops down from the Square, so it meant we were cutting off the residents of the top of the town. The other three, Bolgers, Hughes and Gannon were all together at the bottom of the town close to where Egans Restaurant is now. Also people coming in from the country; Clonad, Raheen, Ballyroan, Mountrath and Mountmellick roads were closer to us.

The building we bought was ideal to be a chemist shop as it had been used for drapery and had plenty of space. Tadgh's previous experience in Carndonnagh helped us in regard to stocking the shop.

Gradually we began to build up a business as we got to know people. I moved from a primary teacher to an unpaid counter hand. We worked from 9:30 am until 8 pm. Unlike now people would come with prescriptions at any hour and during the night. Often we had to get up twice at night time to serve people. Each day began to get busier and then we got an assistant. There were three doctors practicing in the town; Dr O'Connell, Dr McCormack and Dr Owen. They have all passed on. We got to know Dr O'Connell well as a lot of his prescriptions began to come our way. He was the father of Professor F.X. O'Connell, a well-known surgeon in the Mater Hospital. In those days all the doctors were regularly called out at nighttime whereas now the scene has changed.

As I got more involved in the business my yearning for teaching diminished. Our family began to grow with Tadgh RIP, Maura, Paddy, Noreen, Ann and Brendan arriving. Strange as it may seem, none of them were ever interested in the business even to stand behind the counter. It may have been that they saw their father having to get up so often during the night to make up a prescription.

Over the years Portlaoise has changed immensely. Many

shops have come and gone. Across from us was Grants paper shop, which was run by three sisters and a brother. They were a great asset to us so when people came to get their papers we were close by if they needed anything. In our day the town was often referred to as Maryborough but the name Portlaoise was catching on. The two big drapers shops at the time were Shaws and Nolans. There were two hotels, Aird's and Kelly's, which were just three doors down from us. They were the same Kellys as the Foundry and the firm who erected the hay sheds. They did big business all over Leinster. It was a good business town and very competitive.

Working in Shaws at that time was a man from Glenties called George Baskins. He often dropped into the Pharmacy to have a chat and talk about home and occurrences in Glenties. One day he came in and told us he was after buying a house across the way that had become vacant. I wished him well and was delighted, as it would help to develop business at our end of the town. A few days later he was back to tell us that the deal was off as Shaws had stopped his loan from the bank. George later left Shaws and opened a shop back in the North. He would have been related to Bibi Baskin the well-known T.V. personality. George Baskin was really lost in Portlaoise. Back home he was used to going around to dances, football matches and mixing with the people. In Portlaoise the divide between Church of Ireland and Roman Catholic seemed to be greater.

The grocery shops then were Purcells, Hynes, and Whites while Bradleys had a big confectionary shop in the middle of the town.

Our six children all went to the local primary schools. The boys then went to Ballyfin College which is now closed and the girls went to Cross and Passion School, Kilcullen. We had greyhounds in Portlaoise from the word go. The first dog we had was called Willie Wafer. My mother was down visiting us from

Glenties and one night we were discussing the name of the dog and she suggested Willie Wafer - the name on the cornflakes packet. After that we called all our dogs Donegal Fire or Donegal something. My son Paddy last year dropped the name Donegal and some greyhound man from Tipperary has now taken it on board.

Annie O'Donovan and Donegal King in Shelbourne Park after winning four races in a row.

First thing every morning was to gallop the dogs. Tadgh and I would bring them out to a field on the Ballyfin Road, give them a run then we came back and fed them. We then opened the shop and after closing at 8 pm Tadgh would walk out into the countryside - the Abbeyleix Road - with the dogs. We ran them in all the tracks, Thurles, Newbridge, Mullingar, Kilkenny, Harold's Cross and Shelbourne Park. Every night we won was always special. It was a great interest for all the family as they all walked them when needed. For Tadgh, who was working inside in the shop all day, it was a great relief for him to get out at night.

I came to live in Clonaslee in 1987. When the children, who had now grown up, came home on weekends they would say, *'When are you going to give up work'*. So eventually we sold in the summer of 1987. My daughter Noreen had married Donal Sweeney of Clonaslee and was living and teaching there. It was through them that we contacted Jim Sweeney, Donal's father, who was an auctioneer and we bought where we are now. The house needed repair but eventually we got it into shape.

L-R, back row: Donal Sweeney, Annie O'Donovan, Paddy O'Donovan, Sheila Spillane receiving the Champion Bitch Cup in Thurles Greyhound Track from T Dwan, Track Director, John Spillane and P Fielding, Track Director. Front row: Tadgh O'Donovan, Noreen Sweeney, Con Spillane, Shelly Spillane and Mary Spillane with Donegal Burgess.

It was such a change from Portlaoise where we were going all day, hardly a minute to call our own. It took us a while to settle in. It was so different from Portlaoise where we knew everyone and here we knew no one. Having the dogs kept us going. Four years after coming to Clonaslee my husband Tadgh died suddenly. Later Noreen's husband, Donal was to die and he was only forty six.

Paddy, my son, teaches in Rathangan, lives in Clonaslee and has inherited a love for the greyhounds and continues to train them.

In Portlaoise, I used to read books because Patrick McGill, a local man from Glenties, had got me interested. He lived above us in the Glen and became a well-known author. One of his books was banned by the censor of the time. It was cleared afterwards. The title of the book was '*The Ratpit*'. We got it when we were going to school. My sister Mary read it first and passed it on to me. There was nothing in it and nobody in Glenties could understand the commotion and the fuss. At twelve years of age Patrick McGill went to the hiring fair in Strabane. From there he went to work with a farmer in Tyrone. After some time he went to England and then to America. He continued on writing for the remainder of his life. Each year in Glenties they have the McGill Summer School in his memory.

Tadgh and I always kept in contact with Glenties, going back every August weekend. At the moment a niece of mine is living in the home house. The Church where I made my First Communion and Confirmation is gone.

It was an old Church and had gone into bad repair. The new church is very modern. It has within the building a small chapel for morning Mass which I liked. It is very big in area and very high. One sidewall is made of glass, which can be distracting as one can see the passing traffic. The Station Mass in houses is still a feature of religious life in Glenties. People from the surrounding area would come in for the Mass and breakfast would be made for them all. I can still recall some of the townlands: Buncroboy - the bottom of the basket; Strasallagh - dirty homes; Ardun - high hill; Edeninfagh; Meenhalla.

Annie O'Donovan's 94th birthday family get together.
Back row: Brendan O'Donovan.
L-R, Middle row: Niamh O'Donovan, Paddy O'Donovan, Noreen Sweeney,
Conor O'Donovan, Maura Sweeney, Sinead Sweeney.
Front row: Roísín O'Donovan, Martina O'Donovan, Annie O'Donovan, Maura O'Donovan,
Pauline O'Donovan, Orlaith O'Donovan.

I am now twenty years in Clonaslee. Mrs Webster lived next door. It is now Blooms Restaurant. Sweeney's shop was up and running on the other side. Jim Sweeney was managing it and later his son Donal took over. There was a service in the Church of Ireland every Sunday. It is now the Heritage Centre and houses the local library. It is a lovely building. The town has not changed much since we came here. The Vocational School had now moved to its new location. It is a shame that the old building has degenerated into the condition it is in now. What kept us going in Clonaslee was our life with the greyhounds. They had to be exercised morning and evening so I got to know all the mountain roads. I feel that Clonaslee has now gone quiet and appears to be dying. It badly needs local employment. Blooms Restaurant brings people into the town for meals but it does need some kind of industry to give it more life.

My grandchildren now walk the dogs with my son Paddy. And so this family tradition has been passed on.

The world is large but it can also be very small. In Rathangan Vocational School, where Paddy teaches Science and Maths, they got a new teacher recently, in November. At the 11 am break Paddy welcomed him to the school and asked him where he was from. *"I'm from a place a long way from here, you would not know it. It is called Glenties up in Donegal".*

Peter Hogan

My First Car

PETER HOGAN, BROUGHLA

I was always interested in music. My father and uncle and all belonging to me always had a great interest and I must have inherited it from them. My father was a Sean Nós singer. He was always invited to a threshing, a wedding or a wake where he would sing. He also played the concertina. As well as music he was very interested in the French language. On one occasion I remember the guards coming to him as two French people were caught stealing and they wanted somebody to interpret for them. In our house at night time there could be a *house dance* or a *'session'* when other musicians would come. So I was greatly taken up with music from an early age.

My father bought a small melodeon for me when I was about ten years old. I kept at it myself until I learned the notes and mastered a few tunes. The first tune I learned was *"The Wearing of the Green"*. I knew the air of the song so that's the way I began to play. I never took time to learn the notes. When I heard a tune I picked it up straight away.

One day as I began going to the Vocational School in Clonaslee, Paddy Corbet of Ballykaneen was going to Dublin and I went along with him. On arriving in Dublin, on the Portumna bus, which left us outside McBirneys on the Quays, we each went off on our own bit of business. I had to find my way to Waltons, which I was told was up near Findlater's Church, and all it was my first time in Dublin! It was there that I bought a new accordion.

I traded in my old melodeon and paid the balance. I had been saving up for two years to buy this musical instrument. It was a Black Dot Honer, the best make of the time and easy to play. I can remember that day well as Paddy Corbet paid my fair to Dublin as well as paying for my dinner. He was a great friend to me all my life. The first tune I played on the new accordion was the *"The Valley of Loughnanure"*. I was really anxious to see what the accordion was like. It was brilliant. The melodeon was just an ornament in comparison and the sound was much richer, it being a b/c button accordion which gave a lovely tone.

During my years at the Vocational School when the I.C.A. and the Young Farmers were having their monthly meetings, they always invited me to play. Usually they had a cup of tea near the end of the night and I would play a few tunes and some of them would sing along. The I.C.A. had a song:-

Come along and join the I.C.A.
And have a bit of fun
Come along and join the I.C.A.
When your evening work is done

And this would enliven their meeting.

In the Vocational School I had a leaning for carpentry. After school in the evenings I would often stay back as Mr Des Dillon gave me more tuition. I began work as a carpenter with Cantwell Brothers of Kilkenny. One of the first jobs I was on was an extension to Ballinakill College where they were building a new Science Room. At the same time invitations were coming in for weddings and house dances.

In 1947, the year of the big snow, while sliding on ice in a field beside our house, I fell and broke my collarbone. This stopped me playing music for a while. I was in Portlaoise Hospital for five weeks and when my collar bone set I got work driving a lorry for Eamon Bourke, the present Pat Bourke's father who is a local farmer and undertaker in Clonaslee. During the war there was a shortage of firing all over the country. So Eamon Bourke and I became involved in the haulage business. The people around Clonaslee had no work during the war years so they began to cut timber and turf. As a result I spent three years bringing timber to Dublin and turf to Enniscorthy in Co. Wexford. The Dublin County Council bought the timber and turf from Eamon Bourke and it was supplied to the people who needed it in those areas. So I began to know Leinster well. Often I made two trips a day to Dublin. We never had any problems with break downs as Eamon Bourke had two new lorries. So apart from an occasional puncture everything went well. The two lorries were a Ford V8 and a Dodge. I think they are no longer available.

I also did hackney work. In 1940 I bought my first car. It was a second hand Ford 8. I bought it from Joe Dunne who had a garage where Damien Moran is now. I think it was around three hundred pounds.

Peter Hogan on the way to Dublin with a load.

There was no shortage of work. I brought brides to the church. After the ceremony the bride and groom would go home for the reception. There was always a dance in the house after the wedding breakfast and of course I played music the whole day and well into the night. Anybody who had their reception in hotels also invited me in to play. Hayes Hotel in Tullamore was a very popular venue. It is no longer in business. On one occasion in Aird's Hotel, Portlaoise a band let them down so I was drafted in to play.

One must bear in mind that during the war years petrol was rationed. Because I was in the hackney business I was entitled to a certain amount of petrol coupons and as there were very few cars on the road, I was always very busy. At funerals I was always in demand.

Once the Gaelic season started people hired me to go to matches in Limerick, Thurles and Kilkenny. One Sunday on the official opening of Limerick Gaelic Grounds on the Ennis Road, I drove five people to the match. Cork and Tipperary were playing the league final. The famous Christy Ring was playing that day. Cork won by a couple of points.

On the way back coming through a townsland, there was a maypole at a crossroads with a huge crowd present. There was one man supplying the music. So we all got out of the car, the passengers joined in the dancing and I asked the musician would he like a rest. So I took over with my accordion, it always accompanied me in the back of the car and I played a few hours. When I got home there was a dance in Mount Bolus not far from Clonaslee. On arriving there the band was taking a break for supper so I took over. So that was a full days driving and playing. I remember bringing Chris Horan and his father to a wedding in Dublin. The groom was in the bakery business so he supplied the cake and I remember playing at the reception afterwards.

Peter Hogan playing the button accordion with school girl Christina Blake looking on.

I never played in a band as my accordion was always in a different key. But I did play duets and trios. I played occasionally with Johnny Butterfield, who is present leader of the Mount Bolus pipe band. At concerts I played with my family as a group. My son Leo plays the guitar. Raymond plays the banjo and my daughter Yvonne plays the bodhran. So together we often played at parties and in St Vincent's Hospital, Mountmellick for the patients at Christmas. We also, as a family group, with a few more went out with the Wren to play on St Stephen's Day. We went all over Laois and Offaly. We had great St Stephen's Days playing and singing. We had to take off the masks, which hid our identity when we were offered the lovely Christmas cake, turkey and plum pudding.

I was in the hackney business for over twenty years. As more people bought cars the business began to change. I began to bring elderly people to shop in Tullamore and Portlaoise. Sometimes people made appointments in hospital or with specialists in Dublin so I would do a run to the hospital. To have a hackney business one had to have a special license and had to do a special driving test. One had to have a Hackney plate and a special Hackney badge which allowed me to go in to wherever I was driving the vehicle wearing this badge on my coat. When I gave up the hackney business Michael Dunne of Castlecuffe took over.

I then decided to buy a Ford Cortina from local man, Tom Conroy, who had a rental garage in Tullamore. On finishing work in the college at Ballinakill I saw an advertisement in the local paper looking for tradesmen for the new nurse's home and extension to the hospital in Tullamore. So I spent the next five years there until the extension was built. From there I went to work on the new county hall, County Council offices, in Portlaoise. This was another five year job.

While working in Tullamore I began to bring my son Leo, who was a good singer, to Comhaltas sessions. Leo is my second son. I had joined the Killeigh branch of Comhaltas. It was the nearest branch as Clonaslee, as yet, had not set up a branch. A man, John Brady, came to see me while I was working in Tullamore, inquiring would I like to bring Leo to sing at the Fleadh Nua in Dublin. It was the first Fleadh Nua and they have been held in Ennis ever since. Going to Dublin and accepting this invitation was not straight forward. Leo had to perform before a panel of judges in Tullamore to see if he was worthy to be Ireland's traditional singer. Father Pat Ahearne from Kerry was one of the judges. Father Pat Ahearne was in the process of setting up Siamsa which was later to receive International acclaim. Siamsa was to become a big name in Ireland and America, putting on traditional folk dance, capturing life in Ireland around thatching, life at the forge, etc. Father Pat decided straight away to take on Leo. The first Fleadh Nua was presented on Telefis Eireann and was a big success. Later Leo took part in a Comhaltas programme on radio.

I began to go to Fleadh Ceoil's all over the country bringing Leo, Raymond and Marie with me. One year they qualified for the Leinster which was held in Dundalk. Raymond came first in the U11 singing. Leo came first in the eleven to fourteen age group. Marie did the same in her eleven to fourteen age group. That same year Leo went on to win the All-Ireland.

It was decided to set up a branch of Comhaltas in Clonaslee. A meeting was held on the November 24th 1960. The President was Father Fleming, C.C., Martin Fallon was elected Chairman and I was elected Secretary. I held this post for twenty eight years.

The first Fleadh to be held in Clonaslee took place on June 13th 1976. It drew the biggest crowd ever to be seen in Clonaslee. St Joseph's Accordion Band from Portlaoise headed the opening parade followed by the Mount Bolus Pipers Band. The Fleadh was officially opened by Labhras Ó Murchu, Director General of

Comhaltas from a platform in front of what is now McDermott's Pub, it was then owned by Tom Conroy. Throughout the village there were sessions held everywhere. Competitions were held indoors in the Parochial Hall and other venues. Outdoor music was coming from all quarters, duets, trios, small bands and large bands all playing. The day ended with a Céilí in the Parochial Hall, music being supplied by the Bridge Céilí Band. This band had previously won the All Ireland. Its members were from Portarlington, Edenderry, not forgetting Martin Fallon who played both the Uileann Pipes and the fiddle.

Labras Ó Murchu, Comhaltas Ceoltóirí Éireann presenting an award to Peter Hogan.

Clonaslee was to host the Fleadh again in 1977, 1980, 1983, and 1984. In the next decade it was held again in 1993, 1995, 1996, 1997 and 1999. In the millennium year Clonaslee also hosted the event and in 2001, 2002, 2006, and 2007. Over the years many musicians visited and played in Clonaslee including John Brady of Killeigh; Sean Norman along with his céilí band from Edenderry; Denis Gilroy from Kildare; Davey Joe from

Westmeath; Ricey Scully and his band from Tullamore; the Kinsellas from Kinnity. Ricey Scully also recorded the Fleadh live on Radio 3. Through the Fleadh, Clonaslee has now become well known as a centre of traditional music.

Every year somebody is honoured by the Laois County Board for their particular contribution to music, singing and long-time service. I was honoured in 2001. A presentation night was held in the Manor Hotel in Abbeyleix. Music on the night was performed by members of Clonaslee, Camross, Spink and Mountmellick branches of Comhaltas. Johnny Wyer was the 'lone' piper who played me into the hall. It was, for me, an emotional experience meeting people involved in Comhaltas over the years. A lovely mirror bearing my name and the years 1956-2001 along with Waterford glass were presented to me. A unique bronze sculpture of me playing the accordion beside a stove and a fire was also made.

Peter Hogan accompanied by his wife Mary receiving a presentation from
CCE Laois County Board.

As I look back I must thank my family for giving me the opportunity to play and go to so many places. For the past two years I have been able to compete in the traditional singing - being told I was the oldest competitor - and I look forward to competing in the future also.

Margaret Corcoran

Tour de France

MARGARET CORCORAN, BALLINAKILL

"*I will arise and go now, and go to Innisfree*"

W.B.Yeats

I am a native of Co Sligo. I was born in the parish of Calry, which is three miles from Sligo Town. You could now, I suppose, call it part of the city. I grew up on a farm; there were eight of us in the family. My mother ran a little shop so we had people

- Talking Memories -

calling, buying paraffin, tea, cigarettes, bread and all the 'basics'. My father was a Technical Teacher in Grange and so was away most of the day. He was a woodwork teacher. Grange was twelve miles away on the Sligo-Bundoran Road. My father was originally from Grange and so I got to know the area quite well. If Sligo Rovers weren't playing my father would take us to Rosses Point or Mullaghmore beach. You could say Mullaghmore sadly became famous or infamous because of the murder of Lord Louis Mountbatten. He died during the troubles in 1979. All of that area is steeped in history. Drumcliffe where W.B. Yeats lies buried is about eight miles from Calry. My own father and all his people are buried in that graveyard. Local people are still buried there. As children we were all well aware of the epitaph on Yeat's headstone, 'Cast a cold eye on life and death, horseman pass by.'

In the Church of Ireland within the same graveyard there are many stone plaques on the walls referring to the Shaw family who have Rosenallis connections. In Rosses Point there is the well-known golf course where we often played - not golf - because in those days it was very much the gentry who played. Today everybody plays the game. On the other side of Sligo Bay is Knocknarea where according to legend Queen Maeve is buried. In comparison with Croagh Patrick it is not very high and as children we climbed it often. It is a cairn of stones and we were told as youngsters to each bring a stone to add to the cairn.

I was the first of the family to go to the local primary school; Mr Nelson and Miss McGovern were the two teachers. The five brothers and sisters before me went to St Anne's Ursuline Primary School in Sligo and stayed with my aunt who had a hotel in the town. It was called The Grosvenor and was on Gratton Street. My grandmother was from County Tyrone and she met my grandfather on the Derry boat, which was going to Glasgow. They were emigrating to find work. They came back to Sligo after some years and set up the Cruiskeen Lawn Pub in Sligo. They lived there until the 1920's. When my grandfather died my grandmother returned to Glasgow as all her relatives were there. There was no social welfare in those days.

My own mother, Mary Mitchell, would come back regularly over the years on holidays to Sligo. She met my father in the 1930's. They got married in Glasgow and returned to live in Sligo. Our grandmother returned to live with us after the war. From about 1947 to 1958 she lived with us up until she died.

I must say I liked my time in the Primary School in Calry. From there I went to the Ursulines where I spent the next five years. I cycled in most days being only three miles from Sligo. It was all downhill on the way in, so I had plenty of time to go over *'The Acts of the Apostles'* in my head which we had to learn by heart for the nuns. Being from Sligo, poetry was high on the agenda. On Sundays we often borrowed bicycles - there was never enough to go around - and cycled around Lough Gill, past the Isle of Innishfree. It is not a big island about half an acre covered in trees and the poem by W.B. Yeats was one of the first poems I learned. We were always grateful to Mrs Cunningham for lending us her bicycle.

All the nuns in the school were from Sligo and the surrounding area and so they had a great love of history and the locality. The Ursulines also had a boarding school. We all mixed together and so we had Irish native speakers from Donegal, Mayo, Galway as well as girls from Dublin and other counties. I suppose there was rivalry between us but the boarders liked having contact with us. We were the outside world. Altogether there were about two hundred and fifty pupils. One of my teachers was Miss Lee. She was our History teacher. All subjects were taught through Irish. Little did I know that she would have a Clonaslee connection. She was the aunt of Father Robert E. Lee who was a curate in Clonaslee, being on loan from Galway Diocese. Father Robert E. Lee died recently back in Galway. The well-known poet

Padraic Colum visited the school in 1961. He was then eighty years of age. He recited his well-known poem 'The Old Woman of the Roads' and gave us the background story about how he got the inspiration to write the poem. A statue of him is in Eyre Square in Galway. The nuns took great interest in us and were very proud of our achievements. One name that comes to mind is Maureen O'Hara, who later in life became a famous harpist.

The three sisters. L-R: Mary, Catherine and Margaret Corcoran

I left school after doing my Leaving Certificate. I was unsure of what to do and where to go. Mother Philomena, an old nun who was in charge of the day girls, she suffered badly from arthritis, told my friend Angela Keegan and myself that there were two vacancies for untrained teachers in Manchester. So off we set for Manchester by boat. We sailed from Dun Laoghaire to Holyhead. It seemed a big adventure into the unknown. I had only been in Dublin once and here we both were sailing to England. From Holyhead we went to Manchester by train, changing in Crewe. One of the Principals met us in Crewe. The nun had told the Principal that Angela would be wearing a salmon pink suit. The Principal told us she would have glasses. We had an anxious few moments as I never saw as many people milling around looking for different trains going to various destinations. We arrived in Manchester in early morning having changed in Crewe around 3 am.

We began teaching in two different schools. I was in St Mary's and Angela was in St Anne's. We both stayed with the Principal for the first week after which we got our own digs. The children had some difficulty understanding our accent. So we had to adjust, trying to change our vowels. Their surnames were so different from the Irish names we had been accustomed to in Sligo. As history was one of the subjects, we both had to brush up on English history. Every Friday we brought the children down the street to the local church for Confession. We both had First Communion classes. The school was on the edge of Manchester in an area called Ashton-Under-Lyne. We spent one year there. We applied to the Training Colleges and were accepted. However, as Angela had done all her Geography through Irish she was unable to put down the equivalent English terms. So we were separated. She went to Huddersfield to study and I went to Hull. The Mercy nuns were running the Training College so I was back with the nuns again. It was a three-year course. Some of the lecturers were Irish. Sister Dolores looked after the Irish girls. She was from Clare. There were about six Irish girls all from the North. I was the only one representing the south. I kept in contact with Angela, travelling home together on holidays.

Upon completing my training I went back to Manchester where I took up a post teaching in St Edmund's, Monsal Street. Angela got a job teaching nearby. The well-known footballer, Nobby Styles, a member of England's World Cup Team in 1966, was a past pupil.

I took over Second Class. They were seven to eight years

olds. There were about thirty in the class. One of the big events during the school year was the Corpus Christi procession through the city of Manchester. Each child had a special uniform made especially for the big day. It was very colourful. The city stopped for a few hours, traffic being diverted to allow the procession to pass. The annual school tour went to Blackpool by bus, to Southport or any of the seaside towns. During my time in Manchester I met Gerry, my husband, in St Brendan's Irish Club.

In the classroom with Kathleen Ryan, Principal Ann Maher and Margaret Corcoran.

After five years we returned to Ireland. Before coming to Clonaslee, we lived for a time in Rochfortbridge. During this time, I was teaching in Scoil Bhríde in Tullamore. We built our house in

Clonaslee and moved there in 1973. In 1977 I got a teaching post
in the Girls School when Mrs Kathleen Bates retired. The Principal
was Ann Maher; the other assistant was Kathleen Ryan. I taught
Infants and First Class. Cars, of course, have changed everything.
Children walked to schools. There was no phone. Since the
amalgamation the pupil ratio has dropped. More help is available
to children with special needs. When people came to visit us we
said we lived on the outskirts of the village. Now we are in the
village, as it has increased in size with many people living beyond
us out the Rosenallis Road. The new Vocational School moved
from where it was beside us to its new location. Education is now
well catered for. Many businesses have closed. People travelling to
work can now shop further a field.

As our children, five in all, grew up sport was a big factor
in their lives. Gerry, the eldest boy got a bike for his First
Communion. That became his interest from then on. Gerry, my
husband, was a native of Walsh Island where there was a big
interest in cycling. Many from there were members of
Portarlington Cycling Club. The great Alo Donegan was their hero.
Later on when Gerry reached the age of ten, he had to get a
'proper bike'. It had ten gears and was very light. He joined
Tullamore Cycling Club. The categories were Under 12, Under 16,
Junior and Senior. Naturally we became very involved bringing
him to races around the country. Wherever there was a race, be it
Waterford, Cork, Limerick, Carrick-on-Suir or Dublin we were
there.

Gerry seemed to have a natural talent for the sport and
success came rapidly. He won thirty three races in a row. He won
the All-Ireland Under 12 twice, going on to win four All-Ireland
gold and winning silver on the track. The biggest win he had in
Ireland was the Colm Boyd Memorial Trophy, over sixty miles.

He rode as an amateur in France up near the city of
Rheims. He did this for one season before going to America. In

France he won a good few races. He was successful in America where he also broke his leg. In America he was based in Atlanta. He later joined the American Army serving some time in Korea. He was a member of the 82nd Airborne Division.

Gerry became friendly with Sean Kelly and Stephen Roche and so our family started to follow the Tour de France and the World Championship. Through this the Laois Cycling Club was formed resulting in them going to support Sean Kelly, Stephen Roche and Martin Earley in the World Championship. A pattern then developed that our family began to travel to France almost every year to see the Tour. Our favourite location is Alpe d'Huez, which is one of the highest climbs on the Tour. It has twenty one elbows zigzagging to the ski resort at the top. It is approximately 3,350 metres above sea level making it a horrendous climb. The air is so thin that it makes tremendous demands on the cyclists.

Jerry and Margaret Corcoran in the Alps during the Tour de France.

One of our biggest disappointments in cycling was seeing Sean Kelly miss winning the World Championship in Chambery, France in 1989. He came in third. He was favourite to win, missed a gear on the bike and was beaten by a wheel. At that race we met three of the Irish team who had cycled in 1935 with Alo Donegan in the World Amateur Championships. They had cycled from Calais to Chambery - it took them a week - for the race.

One day my husband Gerry met a cyclist who was asking directions for 'The Cut'. Gerry said, *"Why do you want the The Cut?"* *"I am training for Alpe d' Huez later in the year"*, *"Why don't you climb a mountain?"* *"That is what I am doing"* was the reply. *"What gear are you pushing?"* asked Gerry. *"It's seventeen on the back."* Gerry replied, *"You could need at least twenty seven on the back."* He had no idea that Alpe d'Huez was ten times higher.

I spent twenty eight happy years teaching in Scoil Bhríde. One of the biggest advances was the introduction of computers into the classrooms. This happened in the late 1990's.

I was deeply moved and honoured by the naming of the new library in the school after me.

Margaret and Gerry Corcoran at home.

John Flanagan

Give Every Man His DEW

JOHN FLANAGAN, TINNAHINCH

I was very much involved in the organising of the Tinnahinch School Reunion which was held on the December 2nd 2006. Tinnahinch School was built by the local people and the doors were opened on June 1st 1867. In the early days there was a dispute as to where the school should be built, whether it was at Hylands on the Green or the present location. Matthew Maher who lived in Mortimer's house at the time, drew the first load of stones to the present site and this settled the argument. It was mainly a two teacher school with a Principal and an Assistant. In the early days the Principal lived in the school. In the 1940's a teacher's residence was built for the teachers. It is still standing with the Byrne family being the last occupants.

The school consisted of a two room building and *"an bhfuil cead agam dul amach"* was fifty yards down the road in rain or hail. There was no electricity. The classroom was heated by an open fireplace; to what extent depended on how dry the turf was and which family supplied it. Spring water was available from the well across the road. Usually you had to kneel down to get a drink and you were lucky to escape someone pushing you down into the water.

Pupil numbers varied over the years and ranged from a maximum of forty five down to twenty. Classes were from infants to sixth class. The names of the pupils were entered in English in the early days and in Irish from about early 1920's on with a separate register for boys and girls. Full marks to the teachers for the excellent records kept and the copperplate entries made in the register which you can see today.

The teachers in my time were Mrs Twomey, Miss Sammon and Mrs Byrne, with the exception of three years that I attended Reary School. Due to extensive corporal punishment there was a school strike from 1949 -1951 during Miss Sammon's term. Our parents paid Bourke's Taxi Service to transport us to Reary School. The school remained open during that time as there was one pupil in attendance. The dispute came to an end when Miss Sammon retired and we all returned to the school.

The school was then back to full enrolment which at the time was twenty seven pupils. Gradually, like the population of the area, the numbers kept diminishing. Finally the school was forced to close in the month of May 1971. The ten pupils attending the school were then enrolled in Clonaslee and

Rosenallis. The fifth and last teacher was Mrs Byrne who was appointed in 1953. The Department of Education would not appoint a new Principal due to lack of numbers. Her three children, Paraic, Elizabeth and Breda also attended the school and still live locally.

Tinnahinch School had a reputation of turning out very good pupils, many of whom went on to distinguish themselves in various fields. Some joined religious congregations and became school principals. Many had to emigrate to find work. No matter where they went they had a reputation for being conscientious and hard working. This was instilled through their very good teachers down through the years.

Tinnahinch School, 1999

The place name Tinnahinch comes from *"Tigh-na-hinnse"* or *"house of the island."* A fairly large stream flowing into the Barrow at the site of the castle almost surrounds it, creating the impression of an island. The principal castle of the Dunnes was built in Tinnahinch in the old parish of Rearymore, east of

Clonaslee, by Tadhg MacLaighnigh Ui Duinn who ruled the territory in 1475. A map made in 1563 shows this castle, Baun Riaganach, to be near the source of the river Barrow. Tinnahinch Castle was the headquarters or stronghold of the O'Dunne Clan before they moved to Brittas. One of the O'Duinn of Tinnahinch Castle fought at the Battle of Waterloo June 18th, 1815.

Denis Feighery standing at the wall of the original Brittas Castle in Tinnahinch

Tinnahinch Castle when in its glory was a castle of considerable importance and extent. The castle was attacked and blown up by the Cromwellian forces under Colonel Heuston in 1653. There are many references in history to Tinnahinch, such as the Village of Tinnahinch, a fair in Tinnahinch and the Battle of Tinnahinch.

The area of Tinnahinch is approximately three thousand acres, eighteen hundred of which is the mountain. In the 1901 census there was forty one dwellings and one hundred and seventy nine residents. Today there are approximately thirty residents and fifteen dwellings. Tinnahinch existed long before Clonaslee and was part of Rearymore Parish until 1811 when part of the parish went back to Clonaslee and part went to Rosenallis. The west side of the River Barrow went to Clonaslee and the east side of the river went to Rosenallis. The River Barrow was the boundary between Queens County and Kings County. This meant that part of Tinnahinch was in both counties. Clonaslee, at the time, was in Kings County.

Painting of Brittas Castle

In Griffith's valuation of 1851 there were forty families of Conroys and sixty families of Dunnes. The family names in the area are as different as night and day.

The Tinnahinch mountains were a valuable asset to the people of the area for grazing rights, turf and wildlife. In the 1930's and 1940's grouse drives took place but unfortunately the grouse have almost disappeared due to afforestation.

A school reunion, the first and only one, was held on December 2nd 2006 in the Clonaslee Community Centre. One hundred and twenty guests attended at a meal provided by Blooms Restaurant. It was a great occasion with many past pupils meeting some of their classmates for the first time since they left the school.

Past pupils that attended the reunion were in school between 1920 and 1971. The five most senior past pupils were Josie Dunne, May Grogan, Paddy Conroy, Martin Conroy, and Sister Ita Egan who cut the special cake and shared the champagne.

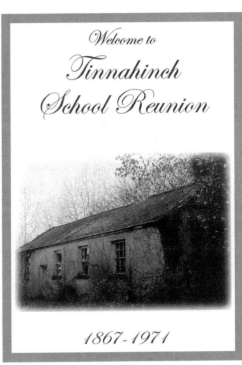

Invitation to the Tinnahinch School Reunion 2006.
Front of programme for reunion.

- Talking Memories -

My father's name was John Flanagan, my grandfather was Daniel Flanagan and my great grandfather was John Flanagan going back to the early 1800's. My mother was May Mortimer, also a native of Tinnahinch. All of them attended Tinnahinch School.

After finishing school in Tinnahinch I went to Knockbeg College, Carlow for five years and completed my Leaving Certificate in 1959. Sometime later I got a job offer with D. E. Williams Ltd. in Tullamore with the help of the Clonaslee branch. I started work on May 1st 1961 with B. Daly Co Ltd in the distillery and the malting section. Bernard Daly was the initial owner of the distillery. He promoted a very able young man who had been working with him for some time, his name was Daniel E Williams, from nearby Mountmellick. His promotion is reported to have given rise to the famous slogan *"Give every man his DEW".* Sometime later he took over ownership, and hence Tullamore Dew.

One of the first and everlasting memories I have was seeing the enormous warehouses and rows of different sized casks of maturing whiskey and of course of the never ending aroma. The wooden casks had names, for example Butts contained 110 gallons, Puncheons contained 80 gallons, Hogsheads 54 gallons approximately. The larger casks were stored on ground level and the smaller were tiered on top. At that time spirits had to be stored in wood for at least five years before it would qualify to be called whiskey. The maturing process has now been reduced to three years by the introduction of smaller and charcoal treated casks. Some casks remained in the warehouse for years; great care was taken vatting and blending to maintain quality and uniformity. All of the casks were numbered and details were recorded by the merchant and the Customs and Excise and had to be accounted for. Both parties had a key to the warehouse and one could not enter without the other. The last time malt and grain whiskey was distilled in Tullamore was 1954.

The great news announced recently is that Tullamore Dew Whiskey is coming back to Tullamore. William Grant & Son, Scotland are about to build a new distillery on the relief road on the outskirts of the town and start producing Tullamore Dew again in Tullamore. During September 2012 they have refurbished the old Bond Store on the canal bank and re-opened the newly designed Tullamore D.E.W. Visitors Centre. They expect to have 40,000 visitors per year over time. I attended the opening and was very impressed with the tour, especially the detail of whiskey distilling and its history. I recommend a visit sometime.

During my time working in the malting division we bought in barley and wheat from the local farmers. The malting barley was grown on contract and was handled through the local branch. When the barley was delivered it was dried and stored, awaiting the malting process. The process first meant steeping the grain in water, after that it was carefully moved along the malt floor to encourage germination. When it reached the kiln it was dried again and eventually found its way to Guinness in Dublin. The feeding barley and most of the wheat was processed in the mill into animal foodstuff, with the assistance of the mill wheel powered by water. At that time, the farmer would get his seeds and fertilizer in the spring on credit at the branch. When the harvest was saved he would "call in and fix up his account" for the year. D.E. Williams had over thirty branches and shops at that time mostly situated in the midlands.

After spending some time in the malting and the distillery, I joined another branch, the Irish Mist Liqueur Company. Irish Mist was founded in 1948 to help use some of the large stocks of Tullamore Dew whiskey. The main ingredients of Irish Mist are whiskey, honey, sugar and herbs. These are mixed or 'compounded' together to make the liqueur. The terminology used is *"brew beer", "distil whiskey"* and *"compound a liqueur".* Irish Mist is a very high quality product and was exported all over the world. When travelling abroad it was a good present to bring with you. Thousands of different size bottles were produced on a daily basis, the labelling and packaging was customised to suit. Quality control and attention to detail is vital when you are in the export business. We received numerous awards over the years that we were very proud of. We were very aware that, indirectly, we were helping to sell Ireland abroad. During my years I met visitors to Ireland from all over the world. I conducted visitors on tours of the plant, I attended the Horse Show, Spring Show, food and drink fairs in the R.D.S. The stand was set up and dressed by the print and design section of the company. Through this I met Noel McMahon who was responsible for founding the *"Tullamore Runners"* an amateur drama group in the town. The *"Runners"* meant that all new comers to the town were welcome to join. The group won two All Irelands in Athlone in the 1950's with Pauric Shelly being one of their star performers. Many years later I was lucky to receive Noel McMahon's pencil sketch of Clonaslee Village entitled *"November Evening 56"*. In all his paintings he signs himself with a dog, in this painting the dog is visible crossing the street.

I spent twenty five years with D.E.W. in Tullamore and as the company downsized and sold off I was made redundant in 1986. During my time working for D.E.W. in the areas of distilling, malting, and Irish Mist Liqueur I enjoyed the challenge that each task brought and I was very sorry to see it close down.

Three weeks after I finished with D.E.W. I was very fortunate to be appointed Purchasing Officer with Offaly County Council in Tullamore. Initially it was a big change as the range of activity for the whole county was enormous. My previous experiences were a great help and I soon got to grips with the job and got to know the people. Very few people would ever encounter the unique range of work experience that I had, working for both the private and public sectors. Everywhere I go, even now, around the county, I am reminded of the many projects and schemes with which I was involved. During that time I procured signs, maps and marker posts for Clonaslee and the Slieve Bloom area. I retired after twenty years' service. I enjoyed working there and made many new friends.

I always kept in touch with Tinnahinch/Clonaslee. I played hurling and football and followed Laois in both grades until they were beaten, then I would support Offaly. Since I came to Tullamore, they have won seven All Irelands, four in football and three in hurling. Because I was born in the part of Tinnahinch that was once part of Kings County, I feel an obligation to support Offaly, but only after Laois have been beaten.

Jane Dunne

American Wake

JANE DUNNE, GLENKEEN/BRITTAS

I was born on May 19th 1916. I went to school in the Girls' School, Clonaslee. My brother Sandy and my sister Mary brought me. Mrs Daly met us and brought me to the desk where I sat. Mary Flynn from Gorrough, Sadie Delaney from Cush, and Kathleen Delaney from Glendine started with me. We lived in Gorrough about two and a half miles from the school. Our next door neighbour had two cross dogs so passing them each morning became an ordeal. Further down the road a sheep came over each day anxious to play with us but we usually went through the adjoining field to avoid him.

Mrs Daly was my teacher in Infants, First and Second Class. Mrs Higgins was my teacher in Third, Fourth, Fifth and Sixth Class. I found school difficult and never liked going back after the holidays. When it was announced in the Church that the school was re-opening after the holidays my heart would sink. The winters seemed to be much colder then. At least that is my recollection of it.

My sister Liz went to work in Kilcormac in the convent and because of her I went to work and study there. I was eighteen and I must have spent three or four years there. My other sisters Kate and Julia got jobs and later got married. My three brothers Jim, Bill and Sandy worked wherever they could find employment. Work was very scarce then, not like now.

After Kilcormac, I came home to help in the house. I enjoyed my time in Kilcormac and was never lonely as I was with my sister. I am the last of my family, the other seven have passed on.

I married John Dunne from Glenkeen in 1952. The best man was Edward Dunne and the bridesmaid was my sister Katie Westman. Father Doyle officiated at the wedding, which was at 8 am. There is no one in the parish anymore by the name of Westman. They have all gone.

After being married, I settled in Glenkeen and we had two children, Margaret and Geraldine. At that time most people travelled by bicycle or walked. It kept us all very fit. At the beginning of our marriage we had an open fire in the house. There was a big hob each side that we could sit on and a big crane came across that held the big and small pot for cooking. We had really large pots for the pig's food and the food we needed for the fowl, turkey, geese and hens. I remember getting a cooker. It was a Stanley 8 and we bought it in Mountmellick. Cooking became a lot easier.

I enjoyed working around the house and the farm, it all came handy to me. I went for water across the field or down the road to the well, which was known as Cusack's well. I reared about twenty turkeys each year and brought them to the market in Clonaslee at Christmas time. We always kept a sheepdog. He was a great help at rounding up the cows and calves. Each year we cut our turf in Glenkeen bog. Everybody did this and the cutting commenced in early spring. One of the first times I went to the bog I remember going over to what was known as Brennan's Rock. It was known locally as a Mass Rock. It is where Mass was celebrated during penal days. I am sure it is still there.

Jane Dunne with daughters Margaret and Geraldine in 1959.

Everybody had a threshing each year. It was a big event. The threshing lasted all day. All the neighbours helped each other. The horses stand out in my mind when I was really young. Threshings were great for us and I drank in every bit of it. There was usually a barn dance that night. It was really great. After the threshing everyone went home and then came back for the dance.

To this day I love the accordion. I prefer it to all the other instruments. My husband John played it and when my two girls were young he would play it in the kitchen. There were also roadside dances. I can remember being at one out the Birr Road.

My father died when I was only four and left my mother with the seven of us. I can remember it, but very faintly. During my early days I never travelled far as there was no transport. When times got a bit better, I went to Dublin occasionally on the bus, which passed through Clonaslee from Birr to Dublin daily. It was too much hustle and bustle and city life was not for me.

In my young days there was a great sense of neighbourliness. The neighbours were always there - through good times and bad. It was safe to leave the front and back door of our home unlocked at that time. I remember our home was one of the many rambling houses in the area. The men folk all gathered for storytelling, almost always ghost stories and after listening to them all night we used to be afraid to go to bed. They also played many card games of twenty five.

It was in the 1980's when we retired from farming and took life easy that John and I moved from Glenkeen to live with our daughter Margaret and son in law Eamon in Brittas. We started to enjoy travelling all over Ireland and in 2004 I went to Lourdes with my daughter Geraldine and her husband Noel and their children, Sandra and John Noel. This was a great experience for me and I enjoyed the trip from start to finish. There is something about Lourdes that makes you feel you want to stay there and forget about home. The whole atmosphere was great and I found a great sense of peace and happiness. We were planning a return trip to Lourdes this year - just before I became ill.

John and Jane Dunne

Knitting and quilt making were great pastimes. I have always loved baking and manys the Porter Cake I made and still make with a recipe handed down to me from my mother. Reading is still my favourite pastime. During my time in Kilcormac I developed a love of reading, thanks to great encouragement from Sister Claver.

Over the years the local branch of Macra na Feirme staged many plays in the Parochial Hall with local people taking part - Sean Mooney, James Costello, Maureen Brophy, Bríd Malone to name a few. A fantastic night out. When Father Ryan was the Parish Priest, a local man, Tom Higgins, presented many slide shows, it was great entertainment. I now enjoy the social evenings in the Community Centre organised by the Social Services with bingo, refreshments and chat. Bridie Conroy and Betty Callaghan organise it. I was also a member of the local I.C.A. for some years. This group has been very active in the parish for many years with great credit to P.D. Brickley, its founder and the many ladies who work to keep it an active Guild. In the 1990's a local group organised guided coach tours of the Slieve Bloom Mountains. Brendan Mahon's bus was always full of travellers leaving Clonaslee for the most interesting and informative tours, passing near Glendine Gap along the J.J. Fanning Pass and many other areas through the mountains. I enjoyed the scenic beauty of these tours very much.

Jane Dunne winning first prize at Easter Bonnet Competition in 2002.

American wakes were once a regular feature of Irish rural life. These wakes were not connected to death but a gathering of family, friends, and neighbours to bid farewell to a young person about to emigrate - more than likely forever. I can remember being invited to one in my childhood. It was at my next door neighbour's house where my friend Mary Ann Flynn lived. She decided to emigrate to America when she was in her twenties. Her parents hosted the wake. There was dancing, singing, eating and drinking. There were tributes of fond farewell and affection to Mary Ann. All the neighbours danced sets, polkas and waltzes to music played on accordions and tin whistles by local musicians. Some people sang songs; others danced the hornpipe or jig. The party broke up just before dawn at which time the neighbours brought gifts and gave them to Mary Ann. They were always small things, because no one could afford much, like rings, small prayer books, rosaries, religious medals and hankies for girls or a pipe for a boy if he was a smoker. After that there were speeches, tears and hugs at Mary Ann's going away. Then her father tackled the horse and cart and took Mary Ann to the nearest station. Crossing the ocean by steam ship sometimes took several weeks and I'm sure there was plenty of seasickness.

I think people enjoy a better standard of living today. They can afford things that my age group could never have afforded when we were young. When I look back on my young days, I did like it - we had good times. We didn't have money but we were happy. I am optimistic by nature so I don't need much cheering up. We should bless each precious moment and concentrate on the happy times rather than dwell on our sorrows. Always take a positive attitude to life.

I now go two days a week, Monday and Thursday to the Day Care Centre in Mountmellick hospital. We get dinner, enjoy concerts and games of bingo. My next door neighbour, Catherine O'Keeffe is the Director of Nursing there.

I have lived through many changes in my lifetime. From the old battery wireless to transistor radio to television. The Tilly oil lamp and candles to electric light. Washing clothes by hand, then the washing board to washing machines and driers. The open fire with large hob on both sides and the large crane hanging over it.

- *Talking Memories* -

Jane Dunne and Eamon Mullins, her son in law, chatting former President Mary Robinson in Áras an Úachterain in 1996.

The baker was a round metal pan covered with a lid. The baker was hung on the crane over the fire to bake the bread. We put coals underneath and on top of the baker lid. Then along came gas and electric cookers and stoves and ranges. Farm butter was made in a churn, now we have wrapped creamery butter. We had unlocked doors in our homes and now we need locks, bolts, monitored and personal alarms. The brown paper bag and wicker basket changed to plastic bags for our shopping. The slane, once used for cutting turf is now replaced by the big machine turf cutters. There were horse drawn hearses now we have the motor driven hearse. There were thatched houses everywhere, now its slates and tiles. We ironed with an old metal block that was heated by the open fire and then lifted out with tongs and fitted into the iron. There were also irons heated by leaning them against burning coals on the fire, then cleaned with paper before

- (223) -

starting to iron. Now we have electric steam irons. Travel was done by walking, pony and trap, bicycles and now it's by the motorcar. The currencies have changed several times, pounds, shillings, pence with the old pound depicting the horseman and plough. Next, the punt and pence, and now the euro. It is now the computer age, there is no comparison with the past.

- Talking Memories -

In front of Sweeney's shop in early 1970's.
L-R: Seamus Conroy, Cyril Morris, Donal Sweeney, James Sweeney.

The Sweeney family. L-R: Jim, Donal, Frank, Maura, Loretta.

Marsh helleborine orchid found in Lough Annagh.

Common spotted orchid found on Eamon
Sammon's farm and Lough Annagh.

King's Bog Orchid.

I.C.A. group photo with Bríd Malone as President in 1962.
L-R Back row: Nuala Young, Kit Barrett, Lizzie Conroy, Bridie Murphy, Kit Murphy,
Mag Dunne, Bridie Murray, Jackie Flynn, Joan Murray, Mary Maher.
Middle row: Eilish Maher, Kit Carroll, Rose Young, Patricia Culliton, Gret Casey,
Merlie O'Keeffe, Rita Fallon, Rita Maher, Lena McCann, Phil Dunne.
Front row: Maureen Dillon, Mary Delaney, Nora Conroy, Bridie Hickey, Martha Flynn,
Bríd Malone, Margaret Dunne, Mary Anne Culliton, Kathleen Dunne, Maura Sweeney.

Fred Mathews home is just 300 years old. The first slated house in the area and still has
its original roof. Inside is a rare stone staircase.

Clonaslee Drama Group. L-R Back row: Ger Conroy, Noel McRedmond, Leo Doyle.
Front: Kathleen Kearney, Alice Dunne, Marie Doyle.

In front of the Post Office with donkey.
Front row: girl with ice-cream, 1) Seamus Foynes, 2) Dinny Kelly
Middle row: 3) Nuala Young, 4) Sean Foynes, 5) Maura Lalor, 6) Tommy Comerford,
7) Eilish Maher
Back Row 8) Breda Lalor, 9) Bridgie Hickey, 10) Joe Hickey 11) Paddy Fitzpatrick.

Sean Ricketts with the pipes and his dog Prince at the metal bridge.

Outside Dublin airport. L-R: Paddy, Tom, Jack and Winifred Blake.

Then

Church of Ireland wedding of Fred and Ena Mathews in 1955.

Now

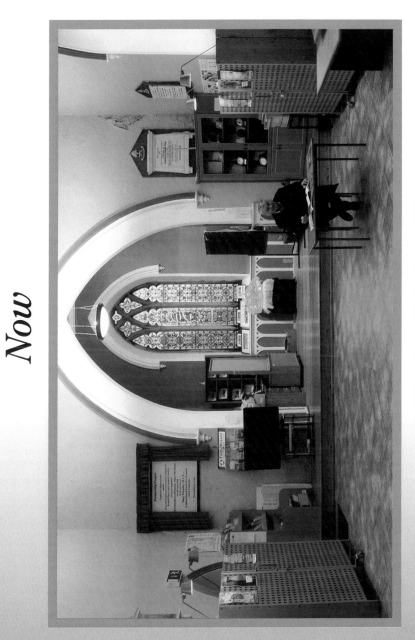

Inside the Heritage Centre with Matt Barrett in 2012.

Then

The village was well remembered by motorist because of the 'acute hump' on the bridge.
This photograph was taken around 1940, note Bill Brien's car 'Hackney' on the far left.

Now

Heritage Centre 2012.

Then

Chatting on the bridge before or after mass in 1910. The building at the back was the branch of D.E.Williams.

Now

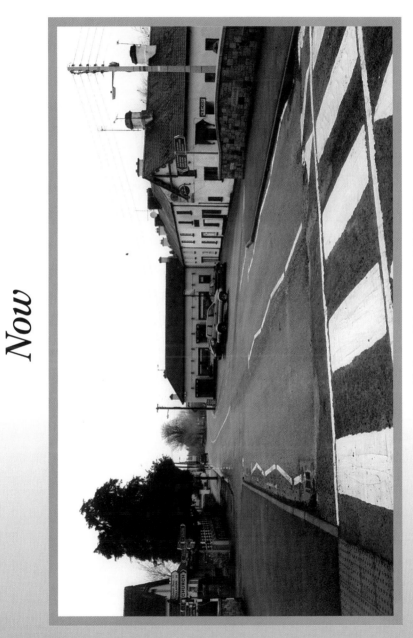

New bridge with Swans Pub and Hickey's Pub 2012.

Clonaslee Senior Hurling Team - winners of Laois Senior Hurling Championship at
O'Moore Park, Portlaoise on October 26th 1975. Final score: Clonaslee 0-13 Clonad 0-8.
L-R Back row: Paddy Delaney (selector), Moling Morrissey, Philip Dillon, William Dillon,
John O'Keeffe (Captain), John Delahunty, Mick O'Loughlin, Paddy Bates,
John Joe Carroll, Mick Lawlor (selector). Front row: Declan O'Loughlin, Fran Bates,
Tom Flynn, Mick O'Connor, Peter McCarthy, Ned McEvoy, Sean Murphy

Father Lar Fleming, a founding member of the Clonaslee Co-op.

Michael Dunne at memorial on Ballinahemmy Mountain in memory of Laois men who died for Irish Freedom during the 1798 Rebellion.

Island at Brittas Lake.

- *Talking Memories* -

West gate into Brittas House at O'Keeffes.

Cutting the cake at the Tinnahinch School Reunion 2006.
Main picture: L-R: Sister Ita Egan, Martin Conroy, Paddy Conroy, Josephine Kelly,
Molly Conroy. Left inset: Mary Collier, Sheila Dunne, Ger Dunne. Right inset:
Elizabeth O'Brien, Breda Fitzpatrick.

Greeting President Mary McAleese at the opening of the Heritage Centre.
L-R Back: Joanne Foynes holding baby Grace, Imelda Cusack, Mary Conroy, Patricia Reddin, Rose Smith, Teresa Burke, Lorraine Daly, Marie Daly. Front row: Denise Smith, Siobhan Conroy, Yvonne Comerford, Louise Cusack, Danielle Cusack, Sarah Egan.

Window in Kilmanman Church.

Margaret Gorman, Bridie Flynn and Ann Flynn greeting President Mary McAleese with
Marie Conroy, Tom Conroy, Sarah Conroy and Mairead McRedmond in background.

The Porpoise submarine at sea.

Dinny Kelly

In the Prisons

DINNY KELLY, COOLNABANCH

$\mathcal{M}$*y first teacher was* Mrs Dunne, she taught me up to third class, before I left her class room she had retired and was replaced by Miss Layng. The school was situated on Chapel Street and had two classrooms. When I moved into the second class room my teacher was Mr John Bates. Some years later we moved to a new school on the Mountmellick Road. After some time Miss Layng was replaced by Miss Cahill, as pupil attendance increased another teacher was employed. A section of the cloakroom was used until eventually an extra classroom was added.

Mr Bates had a big interest in sports, especially in hurling and football. Part of the new school grounds had a grass surface so we could play both games. It was not a full pitch, but an improvement from the old school playground which was small with a hard surface. The school participated in the school championships contesting finals, success never came our way, not in my time. When we practised and played championship games they were in a field called the race course, it was formally part of Brittas estate. The field had a hill on one end which could be to your advantage and disadvantage. Afterwards we played in fields in Caseys of Coolnabanch and in Furlongs of Bellair.

The All Stars - Mick, Nonie and Dinny Kelly.

My father, John had a big influence on me and encouraged me, he had hurled for many years with Clonaslee and held numerous positions at official level. He saw me win my first intermediate hurling medal in 1962. Sadly he passed away the following year. When hurling at minor level I was fortunate to be a member of the county team. At that time it was a frequent occurrence for a club from our neighbouring county to request players to play with their club especially when they reached a semi or final stage. Two years in succession myself and club colleague Billy Conroy of Cush played, illegal of course! Our identity was changed for a few hours on each occasion.

Clonaslee Intermediate Hurling Champions 1962.
L-R Front row: P Delaney, S Finlay, W Flynn, T Fitzgerald, J Finlay, T Flynn, P Dillon, M Fitzgerald, T Conroy, E McEvoy, O Hyland.
Back row: M Maher, J Fitzgerald, D Kelly, D McRedmond, T Foynes, J Hogan, J McRedmond, T Dunne, T Finlay, P Bates, J Barrett, D Gaffney, E Troy.
Final Score: Clonaslee 6-12 to Kyle 3-9.

My brother Mick also hurled at all levels during his school years, he later became goal keeper on the senior team after Clonaslee had won the intermediate championship of 1955. The 1960's were a good decade for our club, winning one junior and two intermediate championships, while also contesting other finals during that period. In 1968 we won the junior, 1969 the intermediate when I was captain and it was a great privilege for me to captain the senior team of 1970 in the county final. It had been sixty years since Clonaslee had previously contested a senior final, regretfully we were not victorious. I think the only club previously to achieve the three titles in succession was Mountrath.

In 1964 I was on the county under 21 hurling team. It was the inaugural year of that championship, we were defeated by Wexford in the Leinster final and they were later defeated by Tipperary in the All-Ireland final. My club colleague Phil Dillon was on the team for the Wexford game. He also played on the county minor team in the All-Ireland of that year against Cork. At the end of the 1960's two of my nephews, John and Richie O'Keeffe, joined me on the team. They collected a senior medal in 1975 when John was captain, a medal I would like to have won, as it is the ambition of all players but I had called it a day by then. Another nephew joined his cousins on the team, Declan Doyle, and he later became goal keeper at senior county level and later played in the Wexford championship. Declan's nephews were in opposition in the Munster Club final 2012, Fergus Kennedy, Crusheen Club of Clare and Paul McNamara, Na Píarsaig Club of Limerick who won the contest, so the tradition is well alive. It is not all about the lads, the girls are competing on the playing fields in football and camogie with their respective counties, Roisin O'Keeffe from Cavan and Aoife Doyle from Wexford. Four other O'Keeffe brothers played with Clonaslee and county, Fran, Denis, Con and Cíaran and in their adopted counties, also successfully claiming silver in club and All-Ireland competitions.

In the sixties our local curate Father Fleming from Carlow organised a parish football league consisting of teams from Clonaslee, Coolagh, Reary and Tinnahinch. I played with Clonaslee, it was hard going. I can't remember who won it out, it was only a one year event. In the early seventies St Manman's Football Club was formed. I was involved as selector and club official. The club has been successful in winning junior and intermediate titles.

School photo: Back: Rita Kelly.
L-R Front: Dinny, Nonie, Mick Kelly.

After leaving national school I enroled in the local vocational school where I spent two years. The teachers were Mr Brickley, Mr Dillon and Miss Touhy. We had no teams in the school but played both codes. When I finished school, I went to work in Salts facory in Tullamore which manufactured textile. Salts employed quite a large workforce, the majority of them were transported by bus from the surrounding villages and towns in Laois, Offaly and Westmeath. In 1961 it reduced its workforce and working week eventually closing down. Employment was as difficult to attain then as it is now.

I applied for different positions including the Garda and Prison service. In the mean time I worked locally at the timber industry and water installation. It was while working at the water installation to five houses on the Tullamore road that I was contacted by the local Garda, Sergeant Walshe requesting to know which entrance exam, garda or prison I was going to choose. As my father had passed away, I chose the prison in the expectation that if successful I may get posted to Portlaoise to be near home.

In 1964 I took up duty in Mountjoy in Dublin, it was nice to meet a neighbour Paddy Kennedy who was in the service for some years. Paddy was in charge of duty detail at the time and facilitated me on match days. Coincidently I became duty detail officer some years after. I was transferred to Portlaoise sometime later, where all the inmates were serving long term sentences, three years to life.

Many of the crimes they committed attracted a lot of public attention, some more than others. One example was a man named Shan Mohangi a native of India who murdered his girlfriend and dismembered her body. He was a medical student in Dublin and in his spare time he worked in a restaurant, the *"Green Toureen"* in Harcourt Street. In the basement of the restaurant he attempted to perform an abortion but failed. In attempting to burn parts of her body the smoke exiting through the grids on the outside footpath attracting passers-by who in turn informed the owners. He was given the death penalty but on appeal his sentence was reduced to manslaughter receiving seven years. He came from a well off family. With less than half his sentence served he was transferred back to Mountjoy and released. He later became an M.P. back in his native country.

Another prisoner, Jas Ennis, on the day he was released from Portlaoise, after serving four years for a serious assault, travelled down to Watergrass Hill in Cork. He assaulted a husband and wife Mr and Mrs Appleby which resulted in one fatality, returned to Dublin and handed himself in. He received a life sentence when tried. In the latter end of his sentence he was transferred to an open institution in Wicklow, where he remains, refusing release.

In the mid-sixties the farmers were incarcerated, they had protested against government policy by holding demonstrations around the country. They were charged with causing obstruction, had to appear in court, fines were imposed which they refused to pay. Subsequently they were convicted and Portlaoise was made available by transferring the prisoners at the time to other prisons, so the farmers had the place to themselves. What a contrast in clientele and daily routine. They were at home on the prison farm, giving useful tips to the farm steward. The atmosphere they brought to the place was a complete change but short lived.

In 1966 I was transferred on temporary duty to Limerick prison returning to Portlaoise in 1967. Limerick housed mostly short term prisoners; there was also a remand section there. While in Limerick I got to hurl with a city team, St Patrick's. On return to Portlaoise I was put in charge of duty detail and in 1972 I moved into the administration area where I remained until retirement in 1998 after serving thirty four and a half years.

Prison officers at site of new Midlands prison. L-R: Martin Costigan, Ronnie O'Reilly, Dinny Kelly, Gus Hayes and Gerry Bradley in September 1998.

I occupy my time since retiring in gardening, saving the turf, sports as a spectator, walking and an odd foreign trip. The townsland where I live joins the townsland of Kilmanman. Situated in this area are the ruins of a church and burial grounds.

In 2008 I joined neighbours Tommy Kelly, Finbarr Rosney and Michael O'Rourke in the clean-up of the graveyard which was seriously overgrown. After some time we were successful in making all areas accessible. During the process I discovered slab stones with names not familiar in the parish for example Turnbull, Dawson, Desmond, Freer, Edgell, Hegarty, and Forster. The church served the areas of Clonaslee, Rosenallis and Castlebrack in the early centuries. Manman was a monk who had a monastery at Lahool on the border of Clonaslee and Cadamstown. He later took charge of the church and became patron saint of Clonaslee Parish.

Tom Foynes

For Whom the Bell Tolls

TOM FOYNES, BALLYKANEEN

I was born in the house beside the Church of Ireland at the top of the town in the townland of Ballinakill. One of my earliest memories is the Church of Ireland bell ringing on Sunday calling the parishioners to prayer. Jack Kershaw always rang the bell. He lived with his brothers Pat and Tom up in Ballinalug. Their house is gone over thirty years. As there were few cars around in the 1940's people came by bicycle and pony and trap. They left their traps in the yard belonging to P. & H. Egan.

I had four brothers and four sisters. I was the second eldest. After finishing school in Chapel Street I went to Ballyfin College for four years. One of my fondest memories is playing for Ballyfin on the hurling team for three years. I was the youngest on the team playing at fourteen for the Senior and Junior team. I have a photograph of myself standing beside Mick Daly, brother of Billy. We won the Senior Leinster College one year beating St Kieran's in the first round and we won the Junior final beating St Joseph's Marino of Dublin. I played full forward. Lar Foley and Des Foley, who later were to become synonymous with Dublin hurling and football, were on the St Joseph's Marino team. Ballyfin were never able to achieve these victories again. Later on I played centre field, number 9, for Clonaslee. In 1962 I played on the intermediate team who beat Kyle in the final. The year before, 1961, Ratheniska had beaten us in the final.

I helped my father out in the building trade. I can remember helping my father lay down a new floor in St Manman's Church in 1958. There was a nine inch drop down from the outside of the church to the flagged floor inside the church. We broke up the flags, poured nine inches of concrete over them. At that time concrete did not come by ready mix, it was mixed by hand. The tiles that are there now were then laid. As far as I remember we raised up the altar rails in order to make the sanctuary higher. My father, Denis, my brother Donal, Dick O'Keeffe and myself completed the work. We also had to shorten the pillars underneath the three galleries because the floor of the church was now nine inches higher. We had to take down the pillars and prop up the three galleries. The pillars in the church are solid pitch pine. They were sitting on a timber base. This was raised up, the pillars were shortened by nine inches and then set back again. New seats - I suppose you can't call them new after fifty years - were also put in. They were supplied by a company

- *Talking Memories* -

from Bagenalstown, County Carlow. The old ones were sold off in an auction in the chapel yard. Standing beside the auctioneer was a brother of Evelyn Cusack, the weather girl on television, Denis, who was about ten years of age. When the auctioneer brought down the hammer after each seat was sold, Denis who had a small stick in his hand would also bring down his own stick and shout out *"Sold again"*. Two years later Father Ryan, who was Parish Priest at the time, decided to take down the old bell, which was located at the apex of the main entrance to the church. The bell was rung by a rope in the choir gallery. Matt Dunne, Kit Murphy's grandfather, used to ring it on Sunday mornings.

The church bell which Tom Foynes brought from Daingean Church, Co Offaly to Clonaslee.

Daingean parish in County Offaly had built a new church and did not require their old bell. I collected the bell in Daingean and brought it over by a pickup truck. A concrete base was laid, bolts were set in the concrete to support the weight of the bell and keep it in situ. First impressions of the parishioners were favourable. The old bell was heard just around the village while this new bell could be heard out in Castlecuffe and up the mountain. The old bell was brought up to Seir Kieran, Clareen Church. I was involved in setting up the bell there. Father Doyle's bungalow on the Tullamore Road was built by the people of the parish and Foynes Construction over a short period.

I went to England in 1965 and worked in London, Birmingham and Liverpool. I always missed home even though there were Clonaslee men working alongside me. Mostly I was building houses. London was my favourite of the three cities. It was bigger and the transport system was better. I was a year and a half working with a builder who had the contract for the upkeep of Barclay's Bank branches all over the city. I got to know London as I was in a different place every week.

Coming home in 1967 I went to work building houses in Wicklow town. I have been involved with construction all my life. From there I got a job in Mountmellick working for Thomas Kelly and Sons who were based in Rathdowney. I stayed with them for almost thirty years. During that time I went to America but when I came home in the winter they always had a job for me.

I found America fascinating. I first went there in 1988 working mostly in Manhatten, New York. The company I worked with were called Golden Vale Construction Ltd. The company was Irish owned, as you can gather by the name, men mostly from Cork and Waterford. They were involved in altering stores after take-overs and reconstruction of hospitals. In one of the hospitals, Mount Sion, we renovated the top floor of the building, the seventieth floor, which was given over to medical experiments on pigs, which was strange to me. I spent six years in America coming home to work in Ireland during the winter. The one winter I did spend in America I found it strange going back to work on St Stephen's Day. This was an eye opener.

Tom Foynes and his wife Noreen outside the White House

As well as building I was always interested in cattle. When I was ten I drove my Uncle Sean Hennessey's cows to the fair in Tullamore. At the back of my mind when I was in America I often thought of coming home and setting myself up with a herd of pure bred cows. In 1980 I bought thirteen acres belonging to Faulkner's here in Ballykaneen. They moved down to Drummond in Rosenallis. I built this house on the land. My son and five daughters have also built their homes on the land alongside me.

In January 1994 I went to visit Seamus Mahon in Kinnitty who had a superb herd of Belgian Blue cows. The purpose of my visit was to get advice from him about setting up a herd of Charolais. But when I saw the Belgian Blues that was the end of my dreams about Charolais. To me the Belgian Blues looked so attractive that I decided to purchase some embryos. Within a month I had purchased eleven from Seamus. This purchase cost me £9,000 which for me was a big gamble and a real act of faith. On November 5th 1994, five cows were born the same day. After that six more came. The following years I began to build up the stock. My idea was to keep building up by selling the bulls and keeping the heifers for further breeding. It was not all plain sailing as several setbacks at calving time happened along the way. I went to Belgium to increase the stock and bought some bulls at a show in Libramont, which is not far from Brussels.

The Foynes family. L-R Back row: Aine, Denis, Josephine. Middle row: Siobhan, Tom, Noreen, Collette. Front row: Mary, Margaret, Geraldine, Denise

In 1995 I started going to shows. The first show I exhibited in was Rathdowney. I won a first, second and third prize. A few weeks later at the Tullamore Show I repeated the same results. So I was on my way from there and I felt that I had made a good choice. The following year, 1996, I really got going exhibiting at shows all over Ireland. Around 2002 I exhibited at Goff's, County Kildare where I also won.

The first All-Ireland I won was in the September Female Class at Tinnahealy, County Wicklow. The following year I won the Bull Class All-Ireland also in Tinnahealy. Also in 1999 in Strokestown, County Roscommon I won the All-Ireland Breeding Heifer. This was the culmination of all my work to breed All-Ireland champions. This gave me great satisfaction winning several All-Irelands in various classes.

Tom and Denis Foynes with a judge at the Tullamore Show in Charleville Estate, Tullamore

My son Denis is also now heavily involved and I am really delighted that he is taking a great interest and being very successful. I gave my grandson Jack a heifer to get him involved.

Starting at an early age, no doubt, he will be bitten as well.

All this involves a lot of hard work. This week on Wednesday I was up in Virginia, County Cavan at a show where we had two winners and a second. Sunday next we go to the Limerick Show.

Even though it is hard work it is very fulfilling, keeping me and my family occupied. They are all very interested and enjoy going to the different shows, especially those that are not too far away.

Bríd Malone

There is No Such Thing as a Small Part

BRÍD MALONE, GARRYHEATHER

I was born in Garryheather, one of seven children, three boys and four girls. I went to school in Castlecuffe and then went to the Presentation Convent, Mountmellick with my sister Anne. Miss Madigan and Mr Dephew were the teachers in the early years and then Mrs Twomey came. Her husband was a doctor. She originally came from Roscrea and they lived out where Dr Sheehan lives now in Clarahill. I loved Irish as we had to do all our subjects through Irish in Mountmellick.

My sister Maura got married so then I had to come home to help on the farm and take Maura's place. Even though I was sorry to leave Mountmellick I had my heart set on farming with the result that I was the only one, out of seven, who married a farmer. On the farm my real love was looking after the cattle, especially show cattle. The Charolais had just come to Ireland. I had a Charolais heifer, which was bred by our own cow and won many prizes. I can remember winning all before me with this animal. She was never beaten at a show and she won many prizes in Tullow, Cavan, Mountrath, Clonaslee and Rathdowney. She won three prizes at the Virginia Show and was Champion of the Show, Best Butcher's heifer and the 10/10/20 Fertilizer prize. There was a picture in the 'Irish Independent' the following day of my son Padraig sitting on the heifer reading the paper with the caption: *"A rest and a read before victory".* The sad part about it was that she got blane, which is a swelling in the abdomen and in the evening time when my husband Joe went up to herd he found her dead on the ground.

In my youthful years I always had an interest in shows. I learned how to make butter from my mother and entered it in the Clonaslee Show. I always reared my own turkeys, geese and guinea fowl and presented them at a show and sale in the old Vocational School in Clonaslee. I also presented jams and cakes at the Show.

I married Joe Malone in 1954, the Marian Year, and we had five children. I named our daughter Marian, because of the year we got married. Our children all went to Castlecuffe National School then to Clonaslee Vocational School up to Inter Certificate. As Clonaslee had no Leaving Certificate at that stage the oldest boys Jackie and Padraig went to Mountmellick Secondary School. The two younger boys, Niall and Fergus went to Ballyfin College.

I got involved in the local drama group at an early age. We put on plays in the local hall and anywhere we were invited. I remember playing the part of Peggy Cogan in the play `The Able Dealer` by Bernard J. McCarthy. The cast was made up of Tom Honan, Carmel Nolan, Joe Malone, Ena Layng, Gussie Ennis, Tim O'Mahony and Sean Mooney. Tom Honan and Carmel Nolan were teachers in Castlecuffe. They later moved to Arklow. They were big in drama in Arklow, reaching the All-Ireland Finals in Athlone. Tom Honan later became a Wicklow County Councillor and became a Drama Adjudicator. Ena Layng was a teacher in Clonaslee. Gussie Ennis worked in P. & H. Egan and later went on to open his own business in Ballycumber. Sean Mooney was a brilliant actor and was really the star of the show.

We also staged `The Whip Hand` by the same author. In that cast was Paddy Corbet, my sister Ann, Mary Hickey, who owns the pub in Clonaslee, and I played the part of Bernie Regan.

Other plays which we staged were 'A Damsel from Dublin' by Thomas King-Moylen; 'Fledged and Flown' by Bryan Michael O'Connor; 'Knocknagow' by Charles Kickham and 'Professor Tim'.

The two plays I liked best were 'Professor Tim' and 'The New Gossoon'. I vividly remember being on the back of a motorbike with Tom Honan in 'The New Gossoon'. The leading roles were always played by Sean Mooney, Paddy Corbet and my husband Joe. I always felt that it was good training as staging a play involves great teamwork. The saying is true, 'there is no such thing as a small part in a play' as each role is so important. The staging of the play involves much behind the scene action. The people who did the lighting, the sound, the costumes and all who helped to build the set, dress the set and front of house people were equally as important as those who faced the footlights. Posters were handmade and put up in all the shops in advance. There were advertisements in the local press and people came early to get the front seats. There was always a great deal of excitement as the opening night drew near and, of course, the curtain was installed and hopefully worked for the opening scene. The group always managed to pay its way and usually at the interval between the acts, tickets were sold for the raffle. We often went to Athlone to see the All-Ireland Drama Finals as two of the former actors, Carmel and Tom Honan, were appearing with the Arklow Drama Group. The group felt strongly that if we had got the same tuition we too would have been capable and would have given a good account of ourselves if we had received a nomination. After all, getting to Athlone meant you had arrived in the drama world and was considered an honours list. Looking back I feel it was a pity that it was allowed to die as there was talent and there still is.

Johnny McEvoy concert in McGinns, Tullamore.
L-R Back row: Anna May O'Keeffe, Johnny McEvoy, Lizzie Conroy, Rose Dunne, Maureen Brophy.
Front row: Mag Dunne, Bríd Malone, Kathleen Dunne.

Farming has changed since Joe and I met. It's a big business now. Then, it was more a way of life and all our neighbours were living off the land. Today many farmers have part time jobs with wives going out to work as well. I know we cannot go back but small farmers are now almost gone and I can foresee the day when there will be large co-operative stores. But I have no regrets as it was a very healthy way of life. We grew our own food and meals were shared with family due to the nature of living together on the farm.

So it was logical for me to join the I.C.A. - Irish Countrywomens Association. My earliest memories go back to 1944 when I joined the local guild. I was eighteen years old and there were approximately sixty-five members in the guild.

Mrs Ena Mathews was President, Mrs Maureen Brophy was Honorary Secretary, Mrs Webster was Honorary Treasurer, and Mrs Sheila Higgins was Vice President. Later I remember Mrs Ena Furlong, Mrs Conroy of Glebe and Miss Gret Casey of Coolnabanch as officers.

We met every month in the old Vocational School. It was really a very vibrant guild and each meeting always provided something interesting: a talk or a demonstration. The meeting concluded with a social half hour. At the same time Macra na Feirme were very strong. They always invited us to their social evenings and we in turn invited them. Great credit must go to Mr Pat Brickley, Principal of the Vocational School, who set up the guild. He was a man of great foresight and vision who saw the value and need of people coming together.

Through the I.C.A. I became involved in many interesting educational projects. It was a great outlet for me as it enabled me to promote the name of Clonaslee far and wide. This opportunity was also available to other women as well.

Courses were available in Public Speaking; Go for Life; Aromatherapy; Tidy Towns; Herb Cultivation; Bread Making;

- *Talking Memories* -

General Gardening; Soup Making; Jam Making. Some of these courses gave me great satisfaction.

ICA outing. L-R Back row: Anna May O'Keeffe, Marie Fenlon, Maureen Cusack,
Anna Snell, Angela Tynan, Breda Conroy, Maura O'Gorman.
Front row: Mary Delaney, Jane Gonoud, Pat Daly, Bríd Malone.

The I.C.A. ran a competition for a Christmas Day menu using roast goose as the main course. I entered the competition and to my surprise my menu came first in the All-Ireland Competition. I felt honoured to be presented with the first prize in Killiney Castle, Dublin, more so as it honoured my local guild and county. In honour of the occasion the guild gave me a lovely copy of William Leech's painting '*The Goose Girl*' which is to be seen in the National Gallery of Ireland.

Our guild gave two half scholarships which entitled the two lucky winners to go for a week to ICA Headquarters; An Grianán, Termonfeckin, Co Louth. An Grianán was donated to the I.C.A. by the W.K. Kellogg Foundation of America of the cornflakes fame. It was donated for *"Educational and recreational purposes*

- (246) -

to promote the health, education and welfare of the people of Ireland". Most of our members frequented courses there. It is in a lovely setting close to Bettystown Beach where participants can walk each evening after classes. It can take 100 people at a time and usually two guilds from different counties go at the same time which makes it very interesting as each guild can exchange ideas and projects. Mountmellick Lace is a popular art course and on one occasion we travelled to Aras an Uachtaráin and presented Mary McAleese with a tablecloth. On a personal note, I enjoyed the gardening and aromatherapy courses very much.

Bríd Malone beside the pump.

I have acted as CDA - County Development Advisor for many years. This has put me in touch with at least seven guilds in the County. My work in this area involves supervising each guild's AGM and encouraging each officer in their role. Also, my work entailed encouraging young women to join the group. It is becoming increasingly difficult to recruit new members with the result that guilds are finding it difficult to continue. As our members get older some guilds have had to close. The ICA was a marvellous vehicle in Adult Education and on one occasion we hosted, in Clonaslee, the ACWW - The Association of Countrywomen of the World.

Sheila Burke obtained a grant for art three years ago and Clonaslee Arts Group came into being. Classes in painting commenced in the Community Centre every Saturday morning. Mary Delaney from Timahoe was our teacher. We are all beginners and we commenced painting what I would call simple and easy objects. At the beginning we learned how to mix the colours and how to sketch. As time went by and we grew in confidence we progressed to painting landscapes and still life. A project started in the County Hall, Portlaoise and our group were each given an item around the village to paint. An exhibition was held of these local paintings: Castlecuffe Castle, The Heritage Centre, former Church of Ireland, Entrance Gates to St Manman's Church, Gates approaching Brittas Castle, Georgian Doorway, Brittas Lake and the Lodge. All of these paintings are now on Clonaslee stone in the Heritage Centre.

Two members of the group have just finished a course in An Grianán in oil painting. The group's work will be on view at this year's 59th Annual Produce and Livestock Show in Clonaslee.

Clonaslee is now awaiting results of this year's Tidy Towns. I was Chairperson for four years and I remember going to a National Conference in Tidy Towns in Kilbeggan in May 1994. Carmel Leahy and I represented Clonaslee. At the conference, when it came to the refreshments I made the remark *"Seeing that we are here in Kilbeggan beside the famous Locke's Distillery where is the Irish Coffee?"* With that there were anxious faces, a hullabaloo, lo and behold up comes lovely Irish coffee which was worth asking for!

Liz Carroll, Maura O'Gorman and I concentrated on the

Outside Blooms Restaurant, Clonaslee with cheque of €1,000 for Laois Hospice from Clonaslee ICA.
L-R Back row: Mary Tynan, Pat Daly, Breda Conroy, Muareen Cusack, Rose Dunne.
Front row: Nora Comerford, Pauline Comerford, Anna Snell, Jane Gonoude,
Laois Hospice representative, Bríd Malone.

cleanliness of the village. We got litter bins from Condrons Concrete and made up hanging baskets. In the middle of the competition of 1996 a Fleadh Cheoil was held in Clonaslee prior to the last judging. Liz Carroll and I went on early patrol at 6 am the day after the Fleadh and when people got up that morning they could not believe how clean the street was. Susie Casey and Ena Mathews always gave refreshments to the workers. We always felt that Clonaslee had great potential because of the Rivers Clodiagh and Gorrough flowing through the village and the Heritage Centre which is a great focal point. When the FAS Scheme came it gave us a break and we welcomed them on board. Last year, Clonaslee took part in *'Pride of Place'*. Clubs in the parish became involved: Foroige, I.C.A., Cómhaltas. Chris Horan did a general review of the area and I spoke on behalf of Tidy Towns.

- Talking Memories -

In the latter years of my life I got the opportunity of travelling. My brother, Tommy Fitzgerald got married in Chicago in the 1970's so Joe and myself went over for the wedding. It was our first time on a plane and of course the opportunity of seeing America was exciting. The skyscrapers made a deep impression and the shoreline of Lake Michigan was really beautiful. It was the month of October; Americans refer to it as the fall, the trees being a lovely copper colour adding to the beauty.

This was the beginning of close ties with America and many trips afterwards. My son Jackie, after his Leaving Certificate, felt that farming was not for him so he decided to go to his Uncle Tommy in Chicago. Marian, my daughter was teaching in Marymount International College in London and during her summer break decided to visit Chicago. She stayed and subsequently got married in America. My other three sons, Niall, Padriag and Fergus were later to follow on in their footsteps. It has to be remembered that in the 1970's there was little employment, farming was difficult and the land could not support four boys.

So Joe and I made many trips for weddings and christenings. Joe had an uncle, Monsignor Patrick Malone, in Iowa and two sisters were nuns, also in Iowa. So our family became acclimatised with the American way of life. Joe loved the trips to America until he fell into bad health. Of course he also loved politics and really loved going to the Fianna Fail Ard Fheis. He worked in Arlington Jewellery for ten years when he retired from farming. He celebrated his eightieth birthday with great gusto in Frank and Veronica Sweeney's High Street House, Tullamore. GAA was big in his life and he was a great follower of Laois.

I am grateful to have such good health, many friends and delighted to be still active in the many organisations that are in the parish. Next weekend I have all my entries ready for the local Show, flowers, cakes, jams and I am not forgetting the turf either.

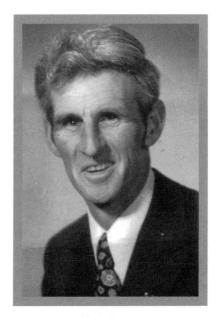

Chris Horan

Where Were We Going to Send the Milk?

CHRIS HORAN, WRANGLESTOWN

My earliest memories of Clonaslee are going to Mass in the Parish Church. We all went by horse and trap. There was a big crowd of us, ten in family and of course we did not all fit in the trap. I am the eldest and was born in 1929. I went in the trap to Mass for a while with my father. My mother might go to second Mass by bicycle, as someone had to stay and mind the house. There was no television then so we had to make our own amusement. There wasn't even a radio at that time. We got a radio when I was around ten years old.

School was not big in my life so I stayed at home on the farm and only attended the Vocational School for a year.

The Parish Priest at the time was Father Murray. I was an altar server and our parents were always nervous as Father Murray was old and very stiff so one of our jobs was to help Father Murray up the six steps that led to the altar. Then the priest said mass with his back to the congregation. Another one of our jobs was to answer mass in Latin. A priest could not say mass then without somebody being present to serve mass. We all learned the Latin responses in the school from Mr John Bates, the headmaster at the time. As I look back we had more of a problem answering the responses in Irish on St Patrick's Day than we had with the Latin. My father and Father Murray were very great and it came as a great shock to them when he was burned in a fire in the Parochial House.

We got a tractor on the farm and we did hire work for people around, ploughing and tilling and trailer work. About 1950 we bought a stone crusher and I worked for Laois County Council. After working for Laois County Council, I worked in Mullingar for a summer crushing stones for the roads. It took longer to make roads then as the material was carted by horses. In 1954, the Marian Year, I went to Toomevara, Co. Tipperary to crush stones as well. From Tipperary I went to Roscommon and from there I came back home to work on the farm.

Pat Brickley was headmaster in the Vocation School and encouraged all young farmers' sons to get involved in a discussion group. These discussions took place one night a week. He set up three groups; one in Kilcavan, one in Killeigh and the local one. At the end of each season we had debates with the other groups.

When Macra na Feirme started I joined along with the whole group. We had a great progressive Macra na Feirme branch in Clonaslee. The group took part in county and national events and it was a great boost to the area.

Chris Horan and Fred Mathews looking after the sow and piglets

It was under the auspices of Macra na Feirme and the I.C.A. that the Clonaslee Show came into being. It was initially held in the old Vocational School. The Show remained there until the Community Centre was built and in the early nineties the Show moved to the present location. It was through Macra na Feirme that the Pig Co-op started. The manager of the National Bank in Mountmellick got involved with us and put up a £100 for a group of us to go and see pig-fattening stations in both the south and north of Ireland. About eleven local people formed a committee to start the Co-op. Some of those people's names I remember, Pat

Brickley was the Chairman and the leading light. Other members were Jim Costelloe, Bill Flynn, Joe Malone, Michael Dunne, Paddy Corbet, Donal Conroy and Fred Mathews, who afterwards became the Manager. Father Fleming the local curate was also very involved.

In the late 1950's and 1960's when I came back from Roscommon to Wranglestown to work on the farm, times were difficult and it was hard to see what one would do on a farm to eke out a living. So in the early 1960's my father and I decided the best thing to do was to go into dairying. The first problem was where were we going to send the milk. Paddy Corbet of Ballykaneen and I visited the Midland Butter and Bacon Company along with others from Clonaslee to discuss the possibilities of starting a branch of the Co-op to take in milk. Donaghmore Co-op in Rathdowney, who had two more branches in Spink and Raheen were approached later. They told us they would take the milk provided we delivered it.

Initially, Sean Young from Kilcavan transported the milk for about two years. After that it was not viable for Sean so Paddy and I arranged transport and brought it ourselves for another year. Then Jim Dunne of Ballymacrory brought it and things went from strength to strength. Milking was done by hand in those days. In 1964 we got our first milking machine and milking parlour. In 1967 I married Betty Doogue from Raheen. We were the first couple to get married in the new church in Shanahoe, in the parish of Raheen.

I was Chairman of Macra na Feirme in the early 1960's when I was approached by Paddy Lalor T.D. from Abbeyleix to allow my name to go forward as a County Councillor. I was co-opted for the remaining two years of the term as I was substituting for Councillor Phelan who had resigned to take up a job with the Forestry.

In the beginning I found it difficult because of lack of time. When the meetings were held in Portlaoise in the afternoon it meant I had to go early to make representations on behalf of people who came to me or else it meant going back on a second day. The farm had to be looked after, cows had to be attended and here was I in Portlaoise, a whole day gone and getting minimal travel expenses. On looking back I often wonder why I took on the job. Anyway it was sorted out in the summer of 1967, when I stood for re-election. I believed that there was no need to canvas as I felt that if the people wanted me they would vote for me. Also I was extremely busy that year, getting married, doing up a house and having to cut silage. I was beaten by a handful of votes but I learned the importance of canvassing.

Chris Horan feeding the cattle

I was nominated again in 1972. That year I canvassed and won back the seat. I ran again in 1977, completed my term and resigned in 1982. Joe Digan of Coolagh succeeded me.

Overall, I found the work of a councillor fulfilling and satisfying. My main difficulty was not having enough time. My family were growing up and I wanted some time at home with them. At the same time I was elected to some sub-committees of the Council, taking up more of my time.

During my time as a councillor I was elected Chairman of ACOT which was subsequently changed to Teagasc and was on the County Committee of Agriculture. At committee meetings discussions took place on farming policy within County Laois. All decisions taken were passed on to the agricultural advisors; the chief agricultural advisor was usually present at the meeting. A Limerick man, Michael O'Connor held the position at that time. He was very up to date on agricultural policy and new farming methods.

I got an opportunity to go to a conference on the Environment and Town Planning which took place in Harringate, Scotland. It was a great opportunity to meet and exchange ideas with other councillors from various Irish counties as well as Scottish and English councillors. One became more aware of how English and Scottish towns were laid out centuries back. In relation to Clonaslee one could see why the Dunnes of Brittas Castle always came to church via the Lodge Gate located on the Green where O'Keeffe's now live. The reason being as they came through the gate they had a marvellous view of the village with the Church dominating the street.

Having a councillor in an area to represent the people is important. During my time we had two councillors in Clonaslee now we have nobody. The other councillor was Paddy Delaney of Coolagh. He represented Fine Gael and we both worked well together on behalf of the people of Clonaslee.

My time in politics gave me some great contacts within Laois County Council, some of which I have retained up to the present. I got great insight into the working of local government and how to avail of grants for local projects.

During our negotiations with Donaghmore we managed to

get eight or nine share-holders in the Clonaslee area. This entitled us to having a member on the Donaghmore Board. At the following AGM I was proposed by Paddy Corbet and duly elected to the Board. I was reluctant to accept the position as it meant more meetings and more work but Paddy insisted whispering to me *'Won't it help you in your*

Chris Horan on the farm up the mountain

political career!' I accepted the position and served for thirty years on the Board. This was a stepping-stone onto the Glanbia Council. While on the Board I got the opportunity to travel to Holland to look at dairy farming in that country. At the time there was talk of Donaghmore and South Tipperary along with other Co-op's amalgamating. This later took place under the brand name Avonmore. We got the opportunity to visit various farms and Co-ops. It was an eye-opener. My first impression was the size and scale of the Co-ops. All the manufacturing was located on the one site. Cheese as well as powdered milk formed part of the output and of course marketing had a European dimension.

On the other hand, Irish farmers had an advantage as we were producing a grass based product. Half of the year in Holland, cattle had to be housed and fed with silage and grain while we had just four months of winter. Eventually I stepped down as Co-op representative after serving on the Council for ten years as I had reached the age limit.

When you get into politics more demands are made on you and so before long I got involved in canvassing for General

Elections. This is really hard work going from door to door looking for support for the prospective T.D.s. I took part in the campaigns to elect Peadar Maher, Paddy Lalor and Liam Hyland. In the recent elections I worked for John Maloney and Sean Fleming.

After leaving the Council I became more involved in community work. A branch of Muintir na Tire started up in Clonaslee in 1972. This really brought me into local affairs and I became active in community projects. There was no piped water to the houses in those days so this became our first project. The Group Water Scheme brought water to people on all roads out of the village. It had to be costed, money had to be raised locally. Grants had to be applied for with local maps and plans being forwarded to the Department of Local Government. Trustees were elected; the only remaining trustee now from that era is Joe Corcoran of Castlecuffe. There was consensus among the people that a local community hall was badly needed. Meetings took place in the Old Vocational School and the Parish Hall, but something larger with facilities for youth was badly needed.

Some felt the Parochial Hall should be extended, others thought this wasn't feasible as there was no off street parking. A site down the Birr Road was looked at, it belonged to Coillte. Eventually Donal Sweeney, being a very active member in the community, approached the Mathews family for the present site.

It is a sixteen acre site located in the townsland of Bellair, presently it houses the new Community Centre, the Vocational School, a soccer pitch, the sports ground for the vocational school, where the annual Clonaslee Show is held, an all weather pitch and also Tír na Spraoi, (Land of Fun Playground).

The building of the Community Centre was a massive undertaking. Before commencing the committee travelled down to Gort, Co Galway to look at their Community Centre. It was there they got the idea of working in conjunction with the V.E.C. This was important as the committee were able to rent the facilities to the school. This has worked very well over the years to the advantage of both. In the early days it was a struggle to make ends meet. A delegation met the Minister of Sport, Mr Frank Fahey T.D. and secured a sizeable grant. The building of the centre fell to local contractor Carroll O'Keeffe. The foundation stone was laid in 1989.

The Centre has been a marvellous amenity not only for Clonaslee but the surrounding localities. The Community Centre was up and running when the Church of Ireland was put up for sale. The Community Development in conjunction with Laois Co Council, decided to buy it. At the time the Community Council had no funds. They had taken out a sizeable bank loan on the Community Centre so the outlook was not great. The County Council made it quite clear that they were not interested in partnership involving a closed building. A positive attitude was needed to make the building come alive and not be just a relic. As the building was in a poor state of repair the Committee and the Laois Co Council applied to Brussels for a European Heritage Grant. This really set the wheels in motion when a grant was authorised for the re-roofing of the Church. Some of the stained glass windows were removed and re-leaded. At this time the community had a very good FAS Scheme supervised by Jerry Bracken. They did great work putting in a new floor, repairing the plaster, which had deteriorated and painting the building.

It was decided to put in under-floor heating and a new Library. Laois Co Council had a branch Library already in the village so now it moved to the more auspicious location. A stipulation in the purchase of the building was that it would be renamed and so it became The Heritage Centre. So it is now functioning as a library, the local Tourist Office and is a centre on occasions for cultural events. Due to its location it commands the village as it gazes proudly down the main street.

Chris Horan with President McAleese at the opening of the Heritage Centre greeting David McRedmond. L-R Back: Eamon Sammon, Mary Kelly, Margaret Conway, Mary Multaney, Alice McRedmond, Margaret Dunne.

In the autumn of 2004 it was decided to clean the spire. However on examination it was found to be in poor condition with a lot of the external stones loose. An architect was commissioned to make a study and report on the condition of the spire. The report found it in a dangerous condition and needing urgent attention. An application was made to the Heritage Council on the basis of the report under the heading of Buildings at Risk. Work was sanctioned to start immediately and a grant was received. The work was to be done in phases and Rainey and Co. Ltd. Steeplejack Specialists from Dublin were employed. This work is still on-going with phase one being completed in 2006.

Most of the projects grew out of discussion at various meetings of the Community Council under the auspices of Muintir na Tire. Muintir na Tire's philosophy was based on the principles of neighbourliness, self-help and self-reliance. It promoted and supported the concepts of active community participation and championed the idea of community development in both Ireland and Europe.

Muintir na Tire's outlook suited a rural area like Clonaslee. With the New Ireland the concept of voluntary work has almost disappeared. More is the pity that it has, as great satisfaction can be derived in working in and with the community. People have less time, we all seem to be so busy and the question of payment and remuneration looms large. It is increasingly difficult to get volunteers for organizations such as Tidy Towns, Community Alert and Community Development. It is more difficult to get volunteers to work for the community since the advent of the FAS Scheme. Clonaslee is not alone in this regard as all other towns and villages are experiencing the same.

With the exception of three or four years during my wife's illness and subsequent death I have been involved in community work for over thirty years. I have no regrets for the time spent in this work. On the contrary I get great pleasure and satisfaction from all the projects undertaken. It is hard to say, as I look back, which gave me the greatest satisfaction. Each one was unique in its own way.

Clifford Mills

Under the Waves

CLIFFORD MILLS, CUSH

My daughter Caroline and I moved to Clonaslee in June 2010. This was the earliest opportunity I could do this for two reasons. The first, due to my wife Mary's dementia, for which I nursed her for fifteen years and the second, the retirement of my daughter from the London Metropolitan Police. I had intended to bring Mary home prior to her death but because of her confused state it was not possible to move. We had been married for forty eight years when she passed away in 2001.

Mary nee Deane was born at Gurteen, Rosenallis in 1919. When Mary was sixteen, she and her two sisters came to Exeter in Devon where they worked in service for a rich family. Our paths were to cross eight years later.

I am a native of Exeter, being born in 1924. I was a very tiny baby weighing just two pounds, barely one kilo. One of my earliest recollections is when I was seven years old in my foster home. I was sitting at my breakfast, when somebody came into the house, took hold of me and walked me down the garden path to a car with an open door. As I was getting in Ma Mills grabbed my arm while another lady held on to me. There was a tug of war. Ma Mills won and took me back to the house. It was only in later years that I discovered my real mother was paying half to the orphanage and half to Mr Mills to keep me but the money ran out. Only for the struggle I would have been sent back to the orphanage. To dear Ma Mills I am forever grateful. Who knows what would have happened to me otherwise.

The years rolled by and in 1938 at the age of fourteen I left school. My first job was house boy at the home of the M.P. Anthony Pershan. I remember going off to be fitted for a suit of clothes. It was a trip to Exeter in a two tone green Morris car. I still remember the journey, the smell of the leather and me, so small, sitting alone in the back seat.

We arrived at the Gentleman's Outfitters, Joshua Davies. I never saw such a sight; new clothes hanging and the smell of camphor. There were several fittings, eventually my new outfit was ready, long black trousers, white shirt and black tie. I looked so smart. I walked home from the village and all of the women were looking out, gasps of surprise, how smart, what a lovely little boy.

My daily duties were long and plentiful. A few of my duties consisted of serving at the table, washing up, general cleaning in the house, taking the master hot water for his shaving, brushing his shoes as well as his jacket, cleaning the fires and many other tasks. My favourite room was the master's study with its thick warm rugs. When the master and mistress were away I spent my day lying on the rugs with the dogs. One day I even tried to smoke one of the master's cigars.

On Sundays I would ride to church with the master and mistress in the pony and trap. They sat in a reserved area of the church. I had to sit apart from them.

From there I went to work for a farmer, Arthur Langdon. I loved the land very much. I enjoyed the freedom but it was hard work beginning at 5 am and not finishing before sunset. Work was all done by horse on the farm. There were no tractors then. When I first started with Arthur Langdon I made friends with a lad named Wally Berry who went off to join the Navy and the Submarine Corps. The changing point of my life came on the day the news came that Wally had perished in the submarine, Vandal. From that moment I wanted to join the Submarine Corps. The Second World War had been running for three years when I decided to join up as a submariner. I did not have to do this as farming was considered a reserved occupation. The troops and everybody had to be fed as the war was taking its toll on the availability of food and farmers were playing an important part in the war effort.

In 1943 I started training on the submarines. The old sailors tried to discourage me as submarines were very dangerous. I was determined to do it, especially for Wally. My first tour was in the Far East. From 1943 to 1946 I served 21 tours on a variety of submarines. Each tour varied from one to three months. Our main job was laying mines in order to destroy enemy fleets. I had many near misses, two of which are more memorable. On the Tally-Ho we were depth charged by the enemy. Initially our submarine had surfaced to fill the air tanks. An enemy ship fired at us, missing the conning tower. Our batteries had run low so we could not dive. We had to make a run for it on the surface. We kept ahead for an hour but eventually had to dive. We went straight to the bottom hoping the enemy would sail over us. This they did but dropped depth charges as they passed over us, one of which pierced the torpedo bay. We were able to keep the water out. We stayed on the bottom for twelve hours eventually surfacing slowly. We limped into Ceylon for repairs.

Clifford Mills joining the Navy at 17 years old.

The second incident was in 1945. I was spare crew on a ship *H.M.S. Adamant.* The submarine *Porpoise* arrived from the U.K. She was short of crew. So A.G. Smith, P.R. Smith and I were all drafted aboard as stokers. One of the main engines had a problem so we spent a few days stripping it down and replacing a piston and big end. We then went on patrol for ten to twelve days laying mines. It was all quiet in the Pacific. On return we went on leave for a few days. Whilst there I was approached by a young man who was also spare crew from the *Adamant.* He told me that the *Porpoise* was to return to the U.K. on the completion of their next patrol. He also told me that his wife had a young baby and she was having difficulty coping with the baby and the fact he was away. So he begged me to let him change places with me. I agreed as I had no compelling reason to go home.

A few days later, early in the morning I watched my shipmates board the *Porpoise,* said goodbye to the crew including my friends P.R. Smith and A.G. Smith. There are many other names which I can't remember. The captain was named Turner. I watched the *Porpoise* sail off. I returned to spare crew duties. The *Porpoise* was never to return. It was never located after being torpedoed. That young man never got home to his wife. I always remember that should have been me.

Every Remembrance Sunday in November I envisage myself standing on the deck of the mother ship the *Adamant* looking and waiting for my friends to come home.

Raising the flag in the Royal Corps of Signals, Parachute Regiment.

I stayed with the Submarine Corps until 1947 when I returned to civvy street back on Langdon's farm. I stayed there until 1950 when I joined the Royal Corps of Signals, the Parachute Regiment. It was during that period at home that I met my wife to be, Mary. She was in service for a military family named Creasey. We married in 1953 in Exeter at the Church of the Sacred Heart. The officiating priest was Father McMee. Caroline was born in May 1955 and her sister Jacqueline in 1956. My wife and I were aficionados of John F. Kennedy and his wife Jacqueline - hence the girls names. From babies the girls were brought to Ireland every year to the home place in Gurteen, Rosenallis. That is where my love affair for the area and the Sliabh Bloom Mountains began. My greatest desire was one day to come home and settle here.

Clifford Mills in front row, third from left with the beret.

I was in the Parachute Regiment for ten years. In 1951 I was made Lance-Corporal and I also got my Parachute Wings on completing my parachute course. In those days we jumped from

600 feet. If your parachute did not open immediately you didn't make it. This happened to several of my colleagues. As we jumped we sang this little rhyme, *"They scraped him off the runway like a pound of strawberry jam. He ain't going to jump no more."*

We did our training in England and then I was posted to Cyprus and Egypt. At that time there was much conflict over the Suez Canal. I was also posted to Australia in the rank of Sergeant. It was while I was in Australia that Mary requested of my Commander-in-chief that I be allowed home to get married.

During my naval career I received citations and medals for serving in France and Germany during the Second World War. I was also the recipient of three Burma Stars; one with the Pacific Bar for my time at sea in the submarines.

In 1960 I was de-mobbed from the Royal Core of Signals. Mary and I decided to go into the catering business. We started running pubs and small hotels. I was involved as a licensee and Mary did the catering. In 1962 I applied for a position as steward of Yelverton Golf Club which was on Dartmoor in Devon. The job involved running the bar and catering for golfers. In my spare time I took up golf myself and got down to a handicap of six which was very good for a late starter.

I stayed there for ten years before moving to Bude in Cornwall to run a pub belonging to a member of Yelverton Golf Club. I was there for twelve years and while the work was very hard I loved it. It was located right on a beach called Crooklets, a beautiful location. We built up a very good business. Mary used to have a fabulous sandwich and salad bar. People used to come up from the beach and take their food back with them. It seemed as if the weather was always very good in Cornwall.

Through my work I met many characters. One was Cyril Grubb. He loved a few pints on Saturday night. I remember one Saturday night he was celebrating a win on the horses. When it came to leaving time I had to walk him outside and lean him against a gate peer and told him to go home. It was a frosty night. At about six o'clock in the morning I drew the curtains back to see Cyril still propped up against the gate posts. He was white with the frost. I panicked thinking I had killed him. But when I went out to investigate he had gone.

Red Island Holiday Camp, Ireland 1963. L-R: Mary, Jackie, Caroline and Clifford Mills.

In 1972 Mary and I along with Caroline and Jacqueline moved to Ferndown Golf Club. It was a rich man's club. Wives were accepted as social members only. Rules were very strict. Dress code was collar and tie at all times except when out on the course. Days were long and enjoyable with plenty of work to be done. The dress code could lead to many embarrassing moments in particular with dignitaries and footballers who believed that because of their status they did not have to abide by the rules. The visiting Chinese Ambassador was one and another was the then Prime Minister Margaret Thatcher's husband Denis who came to play a round of golf and came into the bar without his tie on. I had to very tactfully point out his error asking him to leave the bar until he was properly dressed, namely wearing his tie. His two bodyguards challenged me but Mr Thatcher said *"No, rules are rules"* and he went outside and found a tie. He returned and apologised to me. A week or so later the Captain of the Club received a letter from Mr Thatcher thanking everybody for the lovely day and apologising for the misunderstanding. We worked there until 1982 when Mary started to become ill with dementia. There had been hints and signs over the previous three or four years leading to her inability to run the catering.

Mary and Clifford Mills visiting at Tinnahinch.

I looked after Mary until her death in 2001 over a period of nineteen years. The hardest part was that Mary went from being my wife to my friend. She always used to say *"You are my best friend, you are"*. Our plan had been to retire, do a bit of travelling and to come home to Ireland. In the 90's we came home often looking at houses and places to where we could retire. Mary would get cold feet, panic and the dementia would come on even stronger.

After Mary's death Caroline and I continued to come to Ireland two or three times a year. We stayed in Cush with Noel and Dolores McCann, my niece. Prior to that we stayed with Charles and Betty Deane, Mary's brother, in Tinnahinch. In 2004 we heard that Peter and Betty McCann's house was up for sale. We eventually bought it and the land in 2006 and finally moved to Cush in 2010.

I always loved to walk in the countryside. My legs have become weak so I walk with a frame but Cush gave me the opportunity to enjoy the countryside. I can walk up and down the lane safely in Cush without having to jump out of the way of cars. I love my drives up the mountain, sitting in the car at the Cut, admiring the view, while Caroline walks the dogs. On her return, if it was a good day, we would enjoy a picnic. The most compelling reason for moving here was that I knew Caroline would be safe and surrounded by her family and friends.

I feel I am the luckiest man in the world to end my days here in the care of my daughter Caroline and my wonderful family.